Henry Cowan

The Influence of the Scottish Church in Christendom

Henry Cowan

The Influence of the Scottish Church in Christendom

ISBN/EAN: 9783337239275

Printed in Europe, USA, Canada, Australia, Japan

Cover: Foto ©Lupo / pixelio.de

More available books at **www.hansebooks.com**

SCOTTISH CHURCH IN CHRISTENDOM

THE INFLUENCE

OF

THE SCOTTISH CHURCH

IN CHRISTENDOM

BEING

THE BAIRD LECTURE FOR 1895

DELIVERED IN BLYTHSWOOD PARISH CHURCH, GLASGOW

BY

HENRY COWAN, D.D.

PROFESSOR OF CHURCH HISTORY IN THE UNIVERSITY OF ABERDEEN
AUTHOR OF 'LANDMARKS OF CHURCH HISTORY'

LONDON
ADAM AND CHARLES BLACK
1896

TO

THE MEMBERS OF THE BAIRD TRUST

WILLIAM WEIR, ESQ. OF KILDONAN

WILLIAM BAIRD, ESQ. OF ELIE

JAMES ALEXANDER CAMPBELL, ESQ. OF STRACATHRO, M.P., LL.D.

THE RIGHT REVEREND ARCHIBALD SCOTT, D.D.

MODERATOR OF THE GENERAL ASSEMBLY OF THE

CHURCH OF SCOTLAND

ALEXANDER BAIRD, ESQ. OF URIE

JOHN BAIRD, ESQ. OF LOCHWOOD, AND

WILLIAM LAIRD, ESQ. GLASGOW

WHO HAVE WITH CONSPICUOUS LOYALTY AND EFFICIENCY

CARRIED OUT THE RELIGIOUS AND PATRIOTIC AIMS

OF THE FOUNDER OF THE TRUST

THIS VOLUME IS DEDICATED

WITH MUCH ESTEEM

BY

THE AUTHOR.

PREFACE

THE Lectures which constitute the main part of this volume were delivered last year in Blythswood Parish Church, Glasgow, in connection with the Lectureship founded by the late James Baird, Esq., of Auchmedden, in 1872.

In the religious sphere, the name of James Baird is familiar, chiefly, as that of the munificent donor, during his life, of half a million sterling for religious purposes—a more than princely gift, through which, from year to year, the spiritual destitution of an ever-increasing population is substantially mitigated. But, more valuable than any mere donation of money was the signal lesson which Mr. Baird, throughout his life, impressively inculcated, and of which the gift of half a million was merely the most notable illustration. Alike in words weighty although few, and by deeds many and generous, he taught his fellow-countrymen, and especially the wealthy of his own class, that the possession of capital and the employment of productive labour, no less than the ownership of land and the receipt of rents, entail special responsibility for the provision of religious ordinances and agencies. Mr. Baird did not, as is sometimes carelessly stated, give money to the Church and to ministers. Rather, through money, he gave Church and ministry to the people; to the fresh population, in particular, which he and other capitalists had fostered in new centres of mining and manufacturing enterprise; to the Scottish people also, as a whole, whose already existing spiritual provision it was one great aim of his life to render more efficient for its sacred use. The institution of the Baird Lectureship was one of many evidences which the founder gave that, while keenly alive to the paramount importance of practical Christianity, he was also deeply impressed with the necessity of sound views on theological and ecclesiastical questions.

Along with Mr. Baird, one cannot but here recall his trusted counsellor in the foundation of the Trust and the Lectureship, as well as in all schemes of religious philanthropy—the late Mr. Alexander Whitelaw, M.P. for Glasgow, who gave to the home work of the Church of Scotland much of his wealth, more of his valuable time, more still of his mind and heart. It is no exaggeration to say that in the public speeches, parochial work, and ecclesiastical policy of not a few among the Church's leading ministers, one may frequently trace the development and embodiment of fresh and wholesome ideas which were struck out, like sparks, from Mr. Whitelaw's anvil at Gartsherrie.

The subject of the following Lectures is literally world-wide; for the Scottish Church is more or less represented in almost every region of the habitable globe. The author does not profess to have even nearly exhausted a theme whose ramifications are as numerous as its scope is broad. He hopes simply, in six lectures, to have presented what may be recognised as some instalments of an inquiry which cannot but be in itself interesting to loyal Scottish Churchmen. The lectures, of course, represent merely one side of the relation between the Scottish Church and Christendom at large. The other side, embracing the manifold and varied influence exerted upon the Scottish Church by other Churches—pre-eminently by that of Ireland in early times, and also by those of England and America, of France and Switzerland, of Italy and Germany—has been here only occasionally and incidentally referred to, and merits separate and detailed treatment.

The author's acknowledgments to the many writers, from whose works he has derived testimonies or illustrations, are embodied in the notes. Original and older authorities have been consulted whenever they were accessible. Apart from these, he has been indebted, in the first lecture, mainly to the works of Dr. Skene and M. de Montalembert. In the second, his chief obligations are to Dr. W. Brown's *Propagation of Christianity*, Prof. W. G. Blaikie's *Life of Livingstone*, and Dr. G. Smith's *Life of Duff* and *Conversion of India*. For the materials of the third lecture, he gratefully acknowledges assistance received from A. H. Drysdale's *English Presbyterians*, Professor Lorimer's *John Knox and the Church of England*, and the works of J. S. Reid, Dr. Killen, and Thos. Hamilton on Irish Church History. In the preparation of the fourth lecture, Dr. Burton's *Scot Abroad*, M. Michel's *Ecossais en France*, and Irving's *Lives of Scottish Writers* have been specially serviceable. The facts contained in the fifth lecture have been taken mainly from Prof. Briggs's *American Presbyterianism*, Dr. R. E. Thompson's *Presbyterian*

Churches in the United States, and the earlier works in the same department by Dr. Hodge and R. Webster. In the closing lecture much help has been received not only from Dr. Burton's standard work on the *History of Scotland*, but from W. Burns's *Scottish War of Independence*, in which the direct and indirect issues of the conflict are carefully traced.

In addition to works quoted, the author desires to express his grateful acknowledgment to Dr. Danson of Aberdeen for some valuable hints (embodied in Lecture III.) on the influence of the Scottish Episcopal Church on the Church of England; and also to Professor Paterson of Aberdeen, and other friends, for various much-appreciated suggestions. The index is a young relative's labour of love.

HENRY COWAN.

ABERDEEN, *November* 1896.

CONTENTS

LECTURE I

THE MISSIONARY INFLUENCE OF THE EARLY SCOTTISH CHURCH

Froude's testimony to the "deep mark in the world's history" made by the Scottish people, pp. 1-4; this influence specially notable in the sphere of religion, pp. 4, 5; earliest missionary work of the North British Church — St. Ninian and St. Patrick, pp. 5, 6; Irish origin of the Scottish Church — St. Columba, pp. 7, 8; missionary agency and influence beyond Scotland; I. conversion of pagan Anglo-Saxons, pp. 9-12; II. impulse given by Columba and the Columban Church to Irish missionary enterprise, pp. 12-16; III. indirect influence upon Anglo-Saxon Continental missions in the seventh and eighth centuries, pp. 17-23; IV. Continental mission of St. Cadroe in the tenth century, pp. 23-27.

LECTURE II

THE MISSIONARY INFLUENCE OF THE REFORMED SCOTTISH CHURCH

Missionary shortcoming of Reformed Christendom during the first two centuries after the Reformation, pp. 28, 29; I. early missionary aspirations of the Reformed Scottish Church, pp.

29-31 ; Darien Mission, 1699, p. 32 ; II. establishment of Scottish S.P.C.K. in 1709, p. 32 ; David Brainerd's work and influence, pp. 33-35 ; III. Assembly debate on Foreign Missions in 1796, p. 36 ; contemporaneous foundation of two Scottish Missionary Societies, pp. 37, 38 ; John Love and Charles Grant, pp. 38-40 ; IV. outstanding Scottish missionaries in the present century, pp. 40, 41 ; V. Inglis and Duff, pp. 42-44 ; India at the time of Duff's arrival in Calcutta, pp. 44, 45 ; Scottish combination of Christian education with Western culture, pp. 46-48 ; testimony to Duff's success and influence, pp. 49-51 ; outcome of Scottish missionary method, pp. 52-54 ; VI. David Livingstone, the inaugurator of a fresh epoch in African evangelisation, pp. 54-56 ; opens Central Africa to Christendom, and stimulates African missionary enterprise, pp. 56-58 ; prepares the African for Christianity, pp. 58-60.

LECTURE III

The Influence of the Scottish Reformed Church in England and in Ireland

In England.—Close relations between England and Scotland at the Reformation period, p. 61 ; I. Scottish influence upon the external fortunes of English Protestantism, pp. 61-64 ; II. upon its internal development, pp. 64, 65 ; notable Scottish Reformers in England during the reigns of Henry VIII. and Edward VI., pp. 65, 66 ; ministry and influence of Knox in England, pp. 66-69 ; among English on the Continent, pp. 69, 70 ; III. Scottish influence on English Puritanism after 1560, p. 71 ; English Puritans accused of "Scottizing" during the reign of Elizabeth, p. 72 ; Scottish ecclesiastical influence in England under James VI. and Charles I. ; the *Solemn League and Covenant*, pp. 73-75 ; IV. stimulating example of Scottish Covenanters after the Restoration of 1660, pp. 75, 76 ; influence of Scottish over English Presbyterianism in the eighteenth century, pp. 77, 78 ; in the nineteenth century, pp. 78, 79 ; V. later mutual influence of the Churches of England and Scotland, pp. 79, 80 ; later influence of Scottish Episcopal Church, pp. 80-82 ; VI. Scottish Presbyterianism and English Methodism, pp. 82-84.

In Ireland.—I. Mutual helpfulness of Scottish and Irish Churches in early times, pp. 85, 86 ; II. the Scottish Church in Ireland during the seventeenth century, p. 87 ; (1) Plantation of Ulster and its ecclesiastical issue, pp. 88 - 92 ; (2) Irish Massacre of 1641, and influx of Scottish soldiers and clergy, pp. 92-94 ; Presbyterian organisation in Ireland, p. 95 ; (3) introduction of *Solemn League and Covenant* into Ireland under Scottish auspices, pp. 95-97 ; III. Irish Presbyterianism, how far affected by Scottish, before and after the Revolution of 1688, pp. 97, 98 ; in the eighteenth century, p. 99 ; in the nineteenth, p. 100 ; the Scoto-Irish Church and Home Rule, pp. 101, 102.

LECTURE IV

THE INFLUENCE OF THE SCOTTISH CHURCH AND OF SCOTTISH CHURCHMEN ON THE CONTINENT OF EUROPE

Causes of extensive Scottish emigration to the Continent, especially to France, after the thirteenth century. pp. 103-105 ; I. Richard of St. Victor and Duns Scotus, pp. 105-109 ; II. "Scottish" monasteries in Germany, pp. 109, 110 ; III. John Major and George Buchanan, pp. 110-112 ; Alexander Alane and John M'Alpine, pp. 112 - 115 ; IV. Scottish Catholics on the Continent after the Reformation—Ninian Wingate, pp. 115-118 ; Scottish Presbyterian exiles on the Continent in the seventeenth century—Andrew Melville, pp. 118-120 ; John Cameron, founder of the Saumur School of Theology, pp. 120-122 ; V. John Forbes, the "Aberdeen Doctor," and John Durie, the "peacemaker," pp. 122-126 ; VI. share of the Scottish Church in frustrating the Catholic League in the sixteenth century, pp. 126-128 ; VII. modern influence of Scottish Churches and Churchmen on the Continent, pp. 128-131.

LECTURE V

THE INFLUENCE OF THE SCOTTISH CHURCH IN BRITISH COLONIES, PARTICULARLY IN NORTH AMERICA

I. The Scottish Church in Asia, p. 132: in Africa. p. 133; in Australia and New Zealand, pp. 134, 135; in Central America. pp. 135, 136; II. self-propagation of the Scottish Church in North America. p. 136; derivation of American Reformed episcopate from Scotland, pp. 137, 138; III. predominance of Presbyterianism in North America during the century prior to the American Revolution, pp. 139, 140; extensive emigration of Scottish Covenanters to North America during the period of persecution in Scotland. pp. 140-143; IV. continued Scottish emigration after the Revolution of 1688, pp. 143, 144; influx of Scoto-Irish Presbyterians from Ulster, pp. 144, 145; V. the Church of Scotland recognised as their Mother Church by American Presbyterians, pp. 145, 146; VI. Scottish assistance to American Presbyterianism, pp. 147-149; VII. Scottish and Scoto-Irish ministers in America, pp. 149-152; VIII. Scottish sympathy with the broader section of American Presbyterians, pp. 153-157; IX. the Scottish Church in what remains British North America, pp. 158-161; influence of the Presbyterian Church and of Scottish religious traditions on American Christendom as a whole, pp. 161-168.

LECTURE VI

INFLUENCE OF THE SCOTTISH CHURCH IN THE PROMOTION OF POLITICAL LIBERTY AND SPIRITUAL INDEPENDENCE.

St. Columba's championship of Scottish independence, pp. 167, 168; I. influence of the Scottish Church on the national conflict with England in the thirteenth and fourteenth centuries — prior and preparatory resistance to Anglican ecclesiastical aggression, pp. 169, 170 ; II. patriotism of Scottish clergy in the time of Wallace and Bruce, pp. 170-175 ; refusal of the clergy to endorse the papal ban against Bruce, pp. 175, 176 ; III. indirect influence of the Scottish struggle in undermining royal absolutism in England, pp. 177, 178 ; IV. and in conserving English (as well as French) national independence, pp. 178-180 ; V. the Reformed Scottish Church's resistance to royal despotism—preparatory teaching of Major, Knox, and Buchanan, pp. 181, 182 ; VI. the struggle of the Scottish Church in the seventeenth century, partly against Anglicising policy, pp. 183, 184, but chiefly against tyrannical intrusion, pp. 184, 185 ; VII. inauguration by the Scottish Church of the conflict whose outcome was first the Rebellion, eventually the Revolution, pp. 185-188 ; VIII. indirect influence of the Scottish Church on the downfall of despotism and the development of popular government in Europe and in America, pp. 189-192 ; IX. early testimony of the Scottish Church regarding spiritual independence, pp. 192, 193 ; post-Reformation testimony—in sixteenth and seventeenth centuries, pp. 193, 194 ; in eighteenth and nineteenth centuries, pp. 194, 195 ; X. influence of such testimony in other countries, pp. 196, 197 ; combination of this testimony with the maintenance of Church establishment and of national religious responsibility, pp. 199-202.

NOTES TO LECTURE I. . 203

„ „ II. 208

„ „ III. . 219

„ „ IV. 240

„ „ V. 258

„ „ VI. 273

INDEX 285

NOTANDA ET CORRIGENDA

Page 77, line 15, *delete* ' after Scots'.
,, 151, ,, 1, *for* Purirans *read* Puritans.
,, 226. ,, 13, *for* his work on Church Discipline *read* one of his works on Church Discipline.
.. 255. .. 1, for Francker *read* Franeker.

Addition to Note 35 *on Lecture* III. *and to Note* 24 *on Lecture* IV.

An article by D. J. Vaughan, in the *Cont. Rev.* for June 1878, on "Scottish Influence upon English Theological Thought" refers to Thomas Erskine of Linlathen, John Macleod Campbell, Norman Macleod, and (Bishop) Alexander Ewing, as four Scotsmen whose "influence upon English thought, and more particularly upon English theological thought, has been wide and deep, and certainly will be lasting." Erskine, who spent many winters abroad between 1820 and 1845 exercised also a notable influence upon several leaders of religious thought on the Continent. "Ad. Monod traced to a conversation with him his awakening from his originally Socinian views to the evangelical faith of which he afterwards became so earnest an advocate." See letter of Principal Shairp in Ewing's *Present-day Papers*, Third Series, p. 18. Professor Vinet, of Lausanne, referring especially to Erskine's *Internal Evidence*, wrote : "Were it allowable to say, I am of Paul, and I of Apollos. I should say, I am of Erskine." See P. M. Muir's *Church of Scotland*, chap. x. ; Erskine's *Letters*, i. 366 ; also i. 413.

LECTURE I

THE MISSIONARY INFLUENCE OF THE EARLY SCOTTISH CHURCH

"If we except the Athenians and the Jews," said the late Mr. Froude, when addressing a Scottish academic audience,[1] "no people so few in number have scored so deep a mark in the world's history as you have done."

This testimony may be accepted as not only impartial but indisputable. The wars of Scottish Independence in the age of Wallace and Bruce rank, not only in thrilling interest but in far-reaching influence, with those of ancient Greece against Persia, of medieval Switzerland against Austria, of Holland in the sixteenth century against Spain. In later times the indomitable resistance of Scotland to the despotism of the Stewarts, and the romantic attempts of the Scottish Jacobites to win back for that dynasty the crown which had been forfeited, have in each case enlisted widespread sympathy, and created a fresh department of literature. The patriotic attachment of the Scot to his native land has furnished writers of other nations with an inspiring theme, while, none the less, Scotland has taken a leading share in exploring and colonising the world. Her merchants have been in the van of commercial enterprise ; her emigrants have been most successful, because most persevering and self-adapting, pioneers.[2] In the middle and latter part of the eighteenth century—to take one period as a prominent example—five contemporary Scotsmen each inaugurated a new departure, in more than one case a new era, in European thought, literature, or mechanical enterprise. David Hume became the father of modern philosophical scepticism ; Thomas Reid the founder of that philosophy of common sense through which ultra-scepticism was in that age withstood. Adam Smith, in his epoch-making *Wealth of Nations*, established a new science of Political Economy, revolutionised men's ideas of material prosperity, and preached what was then the virtually unknown doctrine of Free Trade. The masterly work on the Emperor Charles V. by Principal Robertson marks a notable stage in the modern development of philosophical and critical history; while, in a widely different sphere, to James Watt and his inventive genius are mainly due those marvellous applications of the power of steam which have economised human labour a hundredfold, have rendered man vastly more than before the Master of Nature, and, through the locomotive engine (which Watt suggested), have transformed distant peoples into near neighbours. To select three illustrations from the three succeeding generations, the songs of Robert Burns have probably been oftener sung in all parts of the globe, and have exerted a wider and deeper influence over popular sentiment, than those of any other lyric poet, ancient or modern; the Waverley Novels marked an epoch in the history of fiction not only in Britain but throughout Christendom, and have had translators, commentators, imitators, in every language of Europe; Thomas Carlyle, finally, has moulded the opinions and the history of the nineteenth century, and is reckoned among the few prophets of the modern world.

This influence of Scotland and of Scotsmen, notable in almost every sphere, is specially remarkable in that of religion. More or less, doubtless, it may be said of every people that their religious experience and testimony have affected the religious history of mankind at large. "No man liveth to himself"; and no nation worshippeth or worketh for itself alone. But, in the case of Scotland, this truth receives emphatic illustration; and that "deep mark on the world's history" which, in Mr. Froude's judgment, has been made by the Scottish people, is most conspicuous in the signal influence of the Scottish Church beyond the bounds of Scotland. At once in the domain of missionary enterprise and colonial self-propagation, in the sphere of theological testimony and ecclesiastical usage, and on the arena of conflict for civil and religious liberty, the Scottish Church—using that term in the broad sense to denote the entire body of Scottish Christians in successive ages—has occupied a position and exerted an influence in the world far beyond what could have been anticipated from her limited extent, moderate resources, and remote location.

The present lecture will deal with the influence of the early Scottish Church in the extension of Christendom and in the propagation of the missionary spirit.

The authentic history of North British Christianity begins with the record of Potitus, a Presbyter of Strathclyde in the latter half of the fourth century,[3] and of his younger and more illustrious contemporary, St. Ninian, the apostle of Galloway. St. Ninian founded the church and monastery of Whithorn shortly before 400 A.D., and is stated to have evangelised a considerable part of what afterwards became Scotland.[4] The missionary work of this North British church beyond its own territorial sphere dates from the early part of the fifth century. The grandson of Potitus, Succat by name, had been stolen in boyhood from his home near Dumbarton, and sold as a slave to an Irish king in Antrim, whence, six years later, he had escaped. In a vision he seemed to receive a letter with the inscription

"The voice of the Irish," and to hear the cry of the people entreating him to return. In the prime of his manhood he set out to impart spiritual liberty to the land of his former bondage, and Succat, the British slave, became St. Patrick, the apostle of Ireland.[5] His labours extended (according to the general tradition) over more than half a century, and an island hitherto almost entirely heathen became, through his missionary ministry, a flourishing province of Christendom.

The mission of St. Patrick, however, cannot, strictly speaking, be credited to Scottish Christianity, for the Scottish Church, properly so called, had not then begun to exist. That Church had its origin in the latter part of the fifth century, among those Scottish colonists who emigrated from the north of Ireland to what is now Argyll, and from whom our country eventually received its name of Scotland.[6] They brought with them from their Irish home the Christianity which St. Patrick had imparted, and were the earliest really Scottish Churchmen.[7] But the Christian communities then founded were probably neither large nor influential, and, speaking broadly, the history of the Scottish Church as a notable ecclesiastical organisation begins with the advent of the man to whom belongs pre-eminently the designation of the apostle of Scotland—St. Columba.

Few events of Church history are more familiar, at least in their broad outline, than Columba's emigration from Ireland, his settlement in Iona, and his mission to our pagan forefathers. The early date of the two chief memoirs of the saint which have come down —both composed by men who must have known many of Columba's younger contemporaries—enables us to feel that the main recorded events of his life rest on a sound historical basis.[8] We picture his departure, in an open coracle, from his beloved Derry, along with twelve sympathetic companions, in the early summer of 563—impelled to his missionary enterprise partly by remorse on account of bloody feuds in which he had become involved,[9] partly by anxiety to establish better relations between the Scottish colonists in Argyll (men of his own tribe or race) and their pagan Pictish neighbours,[10] but chiefly by the love of Christ and the desire to serve Christ's cause.[11] We imagine his arrival on Whitsun Eve in Iona, then among the most obscure, but ere long to become one of the most illustrious of islands, and his establishment there of a monastic home to which the weary in heart might repair for spiritual rest, as well as a missionary centre whence the active and devoted might go forth for evangelistic labour. We picture the toilsome journeys overland and perilous voyages in fragile boats, made by Columba and his followers in pursuit of their missionary calling; the bold and successful visit to the Pictish King Brude at his fort near what is now Inverness; and the gradual extension of the Christian faith, within the lifetime of Columba or that of his immediate successors, over almost the entire country north of the Forth and Clyde.[12] More than fifty ancient dedications to the saint,[13] from Inchcolm in the Forth and Drymen in Stirlingshire to St. Colm's in Caithness and Sanday in Orkney, confirm generally the witness of early history to the extent and fruitfulness of the Columban Mission.

St. Columba, however, and the Church

which he founded belong not to Scotland only but to Christendom. Within forty years after his death the Scottish Church had entered on her first great Foreign Mission enterprise, and to her influence, along with that of her founder, may be traced, directly or indirectly, a large proportion of the missionary activity of Christendom during the seventh and eighth centuries.

I. We begin with what is most familiar— the influence of the Scottish Church in the conversion of the pagan Anglo-Saxons, who, at the beginning of the seventh century, occupied the greater part of Britain between the Firth of Forth and the English Channel.

In the year of Columba's death, St. Augustine, afterwards first Archbishop of Canterbury, arrived in Kent, sent from Rome by Gregory the Great; and to his labours, along with those of his successors, belongs part of the credit of Anglo-Saxon evangelisation. But the chief share in the honour of having made the Saxons of England a Christian nation pertains not to Rome but to Iona. It was in Iona that Oswald, the royal Saxon saint who reigned over England north of the

Humber, learned, as a boy in exile, to prize the Christian faith, which he afterwards invited his Scottish teachers to impart to his Saxon subjects.[14] It was St. Aidan, the Scottish monk, along with his Celtic associates, who transformed Lindisfarne into Holy Isle, a second Iona, establishing there a monastic and missionary school whence emerged the most successful evangelists of Anglo-Saxon heathendom.[15] St. Cuthbert, the herdsman of Lauderdale, who became the ideal bishop and patron saint of Northern England;[16] St. Hilda, the royal abbess of Whitby, under whom five future Saxon bishops were trained for ministry;[17] St. Wilfrid of York, whose ambitious spirit and Romanising policy were united with genuine missionary zeal;[18] St. Chad, the first Bishop of Lichfield, who consolidated the Church of the English midlands;[19] his brother, St. Cedda, the bishop of what grew into the vast diocese of London, who accomplished what Roman evangelists had vainly attempted, the conversion of the East Saxon kingdom[20]—all these, along with other pioneers and leaders of early English Christianity, were direct fruits of this Scottish mission, which extended itself, in a single generation, from the shores of the Forth to the banks of the Thames. Impartial witness is borne by Montalembert, the Roman Catholic historian of Western Monasticism, to the greater influence of the Scottish, as compared with the Roman Church in the christianising of England. "From the cloisters of Lindisfarne," he writes, "Northumbrian Christianity spread over the southern kingdoms, . . . the influence of the Celtic missionaries reaching districts which their (Roman) predecessors had never been able to enter."[21] He shows how, "of the eight kingdoms of the Anglo-Saxon confederation," four, viz. the two Northumbrias, Mercia, and Essex, "owed their final conversion exclusively to the peaceful invasion of the Celtic monks"; how two of the others, East Anglia and Wessex, "were converted by the combined action" of continental and Scottish missionaries; how "Kent alone was exclusively won and retained by the Roman monks"; and how Sussex, the last of all to receive the Gospel, "owed that blessing to a monk (St. Wilfrid) trained in the school of the Celtic missionaries" at Lindisfarne.[22] Bishop Lightfoot in like manner, with no special bias, one may presume, in favour of the Scottish Church, has declared that, while Augustine of Canterbury was the "Apostle of Kent," "not Augustine but Aidan (of Iona) was the true Apostle of England," and the "Holy Island of Lindisfarne" the true "cradle of English Christianity."[23]

II. The Scottish Church, however, exerted in that early age a missionary power not only directly, through Saxon evangelisation, but indirectly, also, by inspiring churches in other lands with evangelistic zeal. Of Columba himself his early biographer testifies that the lustre of his name and the fame of his work extended to Gaul, Italy, and Spain;[24] while the missionary earnestness of the Irish Church in the seventh century may be traced in part to the stimulating influence of his success in Britain.

There is an old tradition that Columba selected Iona in preference to Colonsay as the seat of his mission because from the latter he could see, while from the former he could no longer descry, his old Irish home.[25] The tradition is embodied in the name which from

time immemorial has belonged to a hill in
Iona—Cul-ri-Erin, "the back turned upon
Ireland." However this may be, the saint
was certainly far from forgetting, or desiring
to forget, the home which he had left, and from
ceasing to interest himself in its welfare.
Repeated visits of Columba to Ireland, after
his settlement in Iona, are recorded,[26] and his
influence continued to be almost as great in
the land of his birth as it became in the land
of his adoption. His powerful intervention,
as a member of one of the Irish royal families,
secured for the Scottish colony in North
Britain an acknowledgment by the Irish of its
political independence.[27] His effective inter-
cession at a critical juncture saved the Irish
bards from threatened expulsion.[28] Monasteries
which he had founded in Ireland prior to his
missionary exodus remained subject to his
ecclesiastical jurisdiction; and his biographer
graphically describes his reception on some
occasion when he visited a monastery in one
of the midland districts. "The entire population flocked out from their farms," united
with the monks and abbot in a long proces-
sion, and "advanced with one accord to meet

Columba as if he had been an angel of the Lord."[29]

On the other hand, Iona received, during the saint's lifetime, frequent visits from leaders of the Irish Church. On one occasion no fewer than four eminent founders of Irish monasteries—Comgall, Kenneth, Brendan, and Cormach—came over together to enjoy hallowed fellowship with Columba,[30] and, indeed, references to visitors from Ireland occur in almost every chapter of his memoirs. Out of 112 saints, moreover, in the Calendar who are reckoned as Columba's spiritual offspring, more than half belong to Ireland.[31] Accordingly, when we meet, towards the close of Columba's life, and in the century after his death, with fresh missionary migrations from Ireland to North Britain;[32] when we find, also, that twenty years after his settlement in Iona a great missionary movement, having continental heathendom as the scene of its operations, began among the Irish monks; when we discover, further, that this movement originated in the monastery of Bangor,[33] whose founder was Comgall, Columba's intimate friend, and that one at least of the most prominent Scoto-Irish missionaries to the Continent—Kilian—had previously been connected with Iona,[34] the conclusion appears inevitable that the personal influence, conspicuous example, and signal success of the founder of the Scottish Church were among the main incitements to that Irish missionary activity.

From Bangor came St. Columbanus, leader of the missionary band, who in the closing years of the sixth century stirred the torpid Gallic Church into fresh vitality, and evangelised pagan Switzerland as well as semi-pagan Burgundy.[35] An Irish follower of Columbanus, in turn, St. Gallus, also a monk of Bangor, became joint founder with him of the Helvetian Church, and has given his name to one of the Swiss cantons.[36] A second Scoto-Irish disciple, Fridoline, became the apostle of Suabia and Alsace;[37] a third, Trudpert, evangelist of the Black Forest;[38] a fourth, the Kilian above mentioned, founder of the Church of Franconia.[39] There is a record of over seventy Irish monasteries (a large proportion of these being founded by Irish Scots), which were established during the seventh century, or soon afterwards, in various parts of the Continent; and each of these constituted a base of missionary operations.[40] There is a parallel record, also, of between two and three hundred Irish saints who in early times were venerated as patrons or as founders of churches in continental countries from Norway to the South of Italy.[41] In that golden age of Irish Christianity, when Ireland was known in Christendom as the "Island of Saints," her Church was recognised as the "Hive of Missions"—a great "centre of Christian knowledge and piety, in the shelter of whose numberless monasteries a crowd of missionary teachers and preachers were trained for the service of the Church and the propagation of the Faith."[42] It was St. Columba mainly who, through the prosperous Iona Mission, opened up to his fellow-monks of Ireland that new world of Christian activity, and thus transformed monastic brotherhoods into missionary regiments. The growth of the Scottish Church, as the fruit of divinely blessed evangelistic enthusiasm and endurance, was the grand fact which Irish continental missionaries were able to hold up before themselves and their followers as an incentive to sustained devotion and an earnest of yet wider success.

III. It was not merely through its reflex influence over Irish Christendom that the Church of Iona became a source of missionary activity on the Continent. To impulses communicated by this Church is also in some measure due the initiation and prosecution of the extensive Anglo-Saxon Mission, or rather series of missions, which culminated in the labours of Boniface, the "Apostle of Germany."

The continental missionary enterprise of the Celtic monks from Ireland was sporadic, although zealous, and their success, while genuine, was limited. Among the Teutons they were aliens in race and speech; in continental Christendom they were aliens in ecclesiastical constitution, usage, and sympathies. They recognised neither papal supremacy nor episcopal jurisdiction, and they adopted, like their fellow-Celts elsewhere, an obsolete Church calendar, a crescent shaped instead of coronal tonsure, and other non-Roman ecclesiastical usages. Accordingly, as in England during the seventh century, so in Germany during the eighth, the Celtic Mission was gradually superseded by the Saxon.[43] Behind the Saxon, however, we find the Scot; behind Canterbury and Rome we discern Lindisfarne and Iona as inspirers of missionary zeal. The pioneer of Anglo-Saxon missions to the Continent was Wilfrid of York, the earliest evangelist of Frisia (the Netherlands) in 678;[44] and Wilfrid, as we have already seen, was brought up at Lindisfarne by St. Aidan of Iona.[45] Twelve years later the work of Wilfrid was resumed, after interruption, by Wigbert, another Saxon, who had been trained in a Scoto-Irish monastery.[46] Two years later still, the Frisian Mission developed, under Willebrord, into an organised Church, with Utrecht as its arch-see; and Willebrord also had been prepared for his life-work in one of those Irish monastic schools which owed partly their missionary direction and devotion to the example of the Columban Church.[47] The ministry of Willebrord, in turn, fired the zeal and stimulated the Christian ambition of St. Boniface, who began his career as Willebrord's helper, and eventually organised a vast missionary diocese extending from Utrecht to Chur.[48] Thus the labours and triumphs of the great Anglo-Saxon Mission to Central Europe may be traced, at least in part, through personal channels to the impulse and influence of the Scottish Church.

The Scottish claim, however, to a share in the glory of Saxon evangelistic enterprise rests on a broader and deeper basis. The missionary zeal of any Church is fostered mainly by the spirit of self-denial and sacrifice, and it was from the Scottish, rather than from the Roman, Church that the early English missionaries received an example of disinterested self-devotion. We have already seen that the mission of St. Augustine, although first in the field, and fortified by the prestige and patronage of Rome, accomplished less for the evangelisation of England than the mission of St. Aidan, which issued, forty years later, from an obscure island in the Atlantic Ocean. The reason is not far to seek. Augustine came to England in the double spirit of service and self-seeking, full of pride as well as of devotion; Aidan came in the spirit of lowly and un-alloyed ministry, after the pattern of Him who lived among men as "One that serveth." When Augustine held his first interview with Ethelbert, King of Kent, he and his forty monks arrived with great pomp, preceded by a verger bearing a huge silver cross; and ere long he accepted and used the royal palace at Canterbury as an episcopal residence.[49] Aidan and his followers, coarsely clad in homespun wool, were content with houses of wood and wattles,[50] and once when he received from *his* king a horse with splendid trappings, he gave it away as a useless encumbrance to the first beggar whom he met![51] Augustine had not long been established in England when he demanded ecclesiastical conformity and submission from the older episcopate of the conquered Britons; his "haughty severity"[52] and threatening language aggravated the bitterness of Celt towards Saxon. Aidan was too much engrossed with "doing the work of an evangelist" to trouble either himself or others with ecclesiastical pretensions or contentions, and his lowly dwelling in Lindisfarne became the common home of men of diverse speech and rival race.[53]

It was under impulses from men like Aidan

of Lindisfarne, rather than from men like
Augustine of Canterbury, that Home and
Foreign Mission devotion would alike be
fostered in the Anglo-Saxon Church, and to
this higher spiritual influence of the Scottish
Mission we have impartial contemporary testimony. The venerable Bede had strong preju-
dices against the Church of Columba on account
of its nonconformity to Roman usage and
Church government. He expresses his detesta-
tion of its non-catholic Easter observance, and
grieves over its irregular episcopate, which,
instead of ruling over the Scottish Church,
was subject to the jurisdiction of a Pres-
byter-abbot.[54] Nevertheless he warms into
eloquence in his eulogy of St. Aidan and of
the Scottish missionaries as a whole. "A
man of singular meekness, piety, and moderation," notable for his "love of peace and
charity"; an "example of self-denial and self-
restraint," who "taught not otherwise than he
lived"; devoted to "meditation and study,"
but "zealous in labour for God"; "superior
alike to anger and to avarice"; himself "in-
different to worldly wealth," but delighting to
use it in "ransoming slaves" and "distributing

to the poor"; stern in "reproving the proud and powerful," but conspicuous for his "tenderness in comforting the distressed"—such is the winning picture drawn by the historian of a rival church and a rival race when he describes the Celtic "Apostle of England."[55] Writing about half a century after the departure of the Scottish missionaries, Bede looks back upon the period of their ministry, notwithstanding their irregular orders and uncatholic usages, as the Golden Age of the English Church. He contrasts their disinterested devotion and laborious zeal with the widely prevalent self-indulgence and sloth of the clergy in his own time, and sums up his impartial praise of the Scottish monks in these comprehensive words: "They were teachers whose whole care was to serve not the world but God."[56] St. Boniface, in his excessive zeal for Roman authority, sometimes dealt harshly and intolerantly with the Celtic missionaries in Central Europe; his unsympathetic treatment of these Scoto-Irish pioneers is the one notable blot on his great career.[57] None the less, his own missionary zeal and self-denial sprang much more from the Celtic than from the Roman influences which co-operated to create and mould the English Church. His organising genius and his Romanising masterfulness Boniface inherited from Augustine of Canterbury, but as regards his grander gifts of missionary earnestness and self-denying devotion, his spiritual ancestors were Columba of Iona and Aidan of Lindisfarne.[53]

IV. One other illustration, less notable, yet not without significance, of the missionary work and influence of the early Scottish Church remains to be described. Three centuries had elapsed since the mission of St. Aidan to England, two centuries since that of St. Boniface to Germany. Continental Christendom, then in the last stage of the first Christian millennium, had reached its lowest depth of spiritual degeneracy and moral degradation. For half a century the Papal chair had been shamelessly filled by paramours or by sons of three abandoned women of the Roman aristocracy; and the moral infamy of Rome had been paralleled by widespread subversion of discipline elsewhere, alike among territorial clergy and in monastic brotherhoods. Here and there, however, were men like Berno and

Odo of Clugny, who sought to stem the tide of degeneracy by timely efforts to reinfuse into monasticism its pristine self-denial and self-devotion. To this continental reform movement the Scottish Church now contributed the work and influence of one of her noblest sons—a kinsman of the royal family, whose name deserves to be rescued from the obscurity of that pre-eminently " dark age,"— St. Cadroe.

No monkish legend, but an almost contemporary record,[50] written, within forty years of Cadroe's death, in the monastery where he spent the eventide of his life, details the history of this Scottish saint and missionary. Devoted from birth, like another Samuel, to God and to the Church by his previously childless parents, who had prayed for offspring at Iona before Columba's tomb, Cadroe was trained as a youth in the monastic college at Armagh, then the chief theological seminary of Celtic Christendom. He constitutes thus the last of many links in a golden chain of mutual intercourse and influence binding together the early Churches of Scotland and Ireland. On his return home, fully equipped with sacred lore,

Cadroe "scattered seeds of wisdom" (to use his biographer's words) throughout the whole country, devoting himself in particular, at his headquarters on the banks of the Earn, to the preparation of Scottish youth for the Church's ministry. After he had thus spent the prime of his manhood, a dream of his uncle St. Bean, in which Cadroe appeared about to pass through three successive caves on his way to a bright shore beyond, was interpreted to mean his destination to a life of self-impoverishment and monastic discipline, along with missionary exile, as the pathway to heavenly rest and reward. Cadroe is "not disobedient to the heavenly vision." In vain the people assemble in crowds to remonstrate against his departure. In vain his royal kinsman, King Constantine, adds his dissuasion to the popular voice. In vain the church of St. Bride at Abernethy, whither Cadroe had retired to pray for guidance, is filled with a congregation who mingle tears with prayers.

> "I hear a voice you cannot hear
>   Which says I must not stay:
> I see a hand you cannot see
>   Which beckons me away."

Eventually the people, under the influence of a monk with missionary sympathies, make themselves partakers of Cadroe's evangelical zeal by devoting to his enterprise rich gifts of silver and gold. And so he enters on his missionary pilgrimage, through Strathclyde to Northumbria, through Northumbria towards London, from London to France. For nearly half a lifetime the Scottish monk exercises his monastic and missionary calling in various regions west of the Rhine, on the banks of the Loire, of the Meuse, of the Moselle; here reforming an old monastery whose discipline had been relaxed, there establishing a new centre of monastic piety, Christian civilisation, and missionary effort. His ministry continued until his death, about 975, on a journey from the Rhine to his home (a monastery near Metz), in the seventieth year of his age and the thirtieth of his voluntary exile.

From one point of view we may be disposed to sympathise with King Constantine and the Scottish people in their conviction that there was as much need for Cadroe at home as abroad. It was a period of political conflict and of ecclesiastical tribulation in Scotland, when pagan Danes and Norsemen, then in the zenith of their power, spread themselves over the northern mainland, and ravaged with murderous violence the shores of the Forth and the Tay. But it became not Scotland, which herself owed so much to Foreign Mission zeal, to grudge in the tenth century, any more than in the nineteenth, the devotion of her best to Christian enterprise in other lands. When Cadroe set out on his missionary pilgrimage, endowed with the substance of his countrymen for the support of his expedition, and enriched with the sympathy which their gifts betokened, both he and they were reproducing the devotion of Columba and Aidan, and were helping to transmit to future ages that missionary spirit of moral helpfulness which is an essential element of Christian character.

LECTURE II

THE MISSIONARY INFLUENCE OF THE REFORMED SCOTTISH CHURCH

The Reformed Churches of Christendom, during the first two centuries of their existence, were not conspicuous for Foreign Mission enterprise. During the sixteenth century in particular, while it would be erroneous to maintain that nothing was done by Protestants for heathendom,[1] the Roman Church, although less evangelical in doctrine than the Reformed, was more evangelistic in practice. For this early shortcoming of Reformed Christendom extenuating circumstances may be pled. Protestant energies were then everywhere occupied, and in some countries engrossed, with the work of self-preservation and of ecclesiastical organisation. Maritime and colonial enterprise, moreover, was mainly in the hands of Roman Catholic Spain and Portugal,[2] so that fewer missionary opportunities were presented to Protestantism than to Romanism, and the spiritual needs of distant heathendom were less prominently brought under the view of the Reformed Churches. Even in the sixteenth century, however, a more substantial beginning of Protestant missionary effort might have been made, and the continued remissness, in general at least, down to the eighteenth century is inexcusable.

I. In proportion to its size and opportunities, the Scottish Church occupied, during that period of discreditable lukewarmness, a relatively reputable position. In the forefront of her original Confession of Faith, drawn up in 1560, the missionary calling of the Church is set forth with a prominence which is found in no other creed of Reformation times. "These glad tidings of the Kingdom"—so the Confession declares in its opening paragraph — "shall be preached throughout the whole world for a witness to all nations." If in Scotland, as elsewhere, this duty of evangelising the heathen was for long practically ignored, it must be remembered that the Scottish Reformed Church, during fully a century of its early history, was in almost perpetual conflict with royal despotism. The Church of Scotland, further, as regards both ecclesiastical emoluments and the condition of the mass of its more earnest membership, was then a poor Church, unable probably to undertake extensive missionary enterprise. Even at the close of the seventeenth century, moreover, little more than one half of the parishes of Scotland were provided with regular ministers,[3] while in the remoter Highlands and Islands, destitute to a great extent of religious ordinances, there was practically a Foreign Mission field at the Church's own door, claiming priority of attention and cultivation.

About the close of the sixteenth century, during a brief period of ecclesiastical tranquillity, missionary operations were inaugurated north of Inverness and also in Lewis,[4] but the work was unhappily arrested (apart from local hindrances) by the anglicising policy of King James, and the protracted strife which ensued. Half a century later, in 1647, the same Assembly which approved the Westminster Confession of Faith recognised in the restoration of the Church's liberties a providential call to missionary effort. "Since the mighty and outstretched arm of the Lord"—so that Assembly declares—"hath brought us out of Egypt, and restored to us well-constituted and free national synods, it hath been our desire and endeavour to set forward the Kingdom of our Lord Jesus Christ not only throughout this nation, but in other parts also, so far as God may open to us the way."[5] Once more, however, the conflicts of the Church, first with Oliver Cromwell, and subsequently with the restored monarchy, prevented these aspirations from being realised. Nine years after the Revolution Settlement of 1690, when the Scottish Church had at length entered on a period of comparative peace and prosperity, the first practical step was taken in the direction of Foreign Mission enterprise, at a time when Reformed Christendom as a whole still slumbered as regards missionary obligations. The occasion was supplied by the famous

Darien expedition in 1698. Ten Presbyterian ministers accompanied the colonists, and were enjoined by the General Assembly to labour not only among their fellow-countrymen, but among the heathen natives. A pastoral letter was despatched in 1700 expressing the devout hope that "the Lord would yet honour the missionary ministers and the Church from which they had been sent to carry His name among the heathen."[6] One of the ten was the notable Covenanter, Alexander Shields, the friend and biographer of James Renwick, the martyr.[7]

II. With the collapse of the ill-fated Darien scheme the mission came also to an end, but a few years later, in 1709, was constituted the Scottish Society for the Propagation of Christian Knowledge, with whose work the modern history of Scottish Foreign Missions practically begins. The main field, indeed, of that Society was among the Gaelic population at home, but a mission to the North American Indians was also established. The third labourer in this field, appointed in 1743, was the illustrious David Brainerd.[8]

The missionary career of Brainerd, short though it was (he died after four years' service), marks an era both in the annals of American Indian evangelisation and in the general history of Protestant missionary enterprise. There were eminent missionaries, indeed, to the Indians of North America long anterior to Brainerd. Before the middle of the seventeenth century two English Puritans, John Eliot and Thomas Mayhew, had begun their apostolic labours among the native tribes of Massachusetts, who received from the former the Indian Bible.[9] But the work of these pioneers had not been adequately followed up, and when the Scottish Society entered the field, the enterprise had practically to be commenced anew. To David Brainerd, himself an American by birth, but none the less an ambassador of the Scottish Church, belongs the chief honour of having awakened American Christendom to a genuine sense of responsibility for the religious condition of those native tribes whom British colonisation had gradually displaced.[10] His student life had been contemporaneous with a spiritual awakening, which had developed during a visit of George Whitefield into a signal revival ; and the enthusiasm of devotion, which the great English evangelist had kindled and diffused, manifested itself, in Brainerd's case, as a missionary fervour. His chivalrous declinature of repeated calls to attractive spheres of pastoral labour, and his disinterested devotion of high intellectual gifts to the despised Red men ; his four years' arduous ministry, without colleague or even (for a portion of the time) civilised companionship, among the native populations of Massachusetts, Pennsylvania, and New Jersey; his perils and privations, cheerfully undergone, in a floorless log-cabin, with a heap of straw for his bed and boiled corn for his fare ; his constant journeys through forest wilds, amid exposure to rain and cold, as well as frequent prostration by fever and ague when far from medical aid ; the encouraging success and early fruits[11] of his labours among "my poor Indians," who were then widely regarded as impervious to Christian truth ; the disuse by entire communities, under his influence, of idolatrous sacrifice, flagrant intemperance, and a facility

of divorce involving virtual profligacy; the
conspicuous steadfastness, finally, after his
death, of the comparative few to whom, after
a thorough testing, he felt himself justified
in administering baptism [12]—all this constituted a moral force which exerted a twofold influence on missionary enterprise. On
the one hand, in the narrower sphere of
American Christian activity, there resulted
(eventually at least) a more sustained and
systematic effort to evangelise the red man,
through missionary operations which have
tempered the frequent selfishness of American
political dealings with the race, and have
issued in a large portion of the remanent
Indian population being Christianised.[13] On
the other hand, in the wider sphere of the
Reformed Church at large, seeds of missionary
influence were sown which afterwards yielded
a fruitful harvest. Amid the evangelical and
evangelistic revival in the beginning of the
present century, when missionary literature,
now abundant and stimulating, was scant and
ineffective, no missionary biography so often
kindled in the souls of future labourers a
missionary zeal, or so much sustained their

hearts afterwards in difficulty and discouragement, as Jonathan Edwards's *Life*—virtually an autobiography — *of David Brainerd*. Through his Indian ministry Scotland served well the missionary cause, not only in his own, but in later times, and not merely in America, but throughout Reformed Christendom.[14]

III. About half a century after David Brainerd's death, a long discussion on Foreign Missions took place in the General Assembly of the Church of Scotland. It was the memorable debate of 1796, in the course of which the venerable John Erskine of Greyfriars' Church, Edinburgh—the Erskine immortalised in *Guy Mannering*[15]—replied to an anti-missionary speech with the significant demand, "Moderator, rax (reach) me that Bible." The discussion resulted in the rejection of two synodical overtures, which had proposed that the Assembly should organise a Foreign Mission; and this unfortunate issue has often been quoted as an illustration of the backwardness of the Scottish Church, a century ago, in the fulfilment of her Divine Captain's "marching orders." With equal propriety it might be adduced as an evidence of Scotland's comparative forwardness in missionary zeal; for the motion to establish a Foreign Mission of the Church was lost by a majority of only 14 in a house of 102 members; while the resolution adopted was grounded merely on temporary inexpediency, and declared the Church's readiness to "embrace with zeal and with thankfulness any favourable opportunity of contributing to the propagation of the Gospel of Christ which Divine Providence may hereafter open."[16] Probably at that time there was no other Reformed Church in Europe, except the Moravian,[17] whose Supreme Court or Council would have shown a minority so large in favour of official and immediate missionary action. In the very year of this notable Assembly, evidence of widespread sympathy with the cause was supplied by the foundation of two Scottish Missionary Societies, one in Edinburgh,[18] the other in Glasgow.[19] Both these associations were composed of office-bearers and members of the Church of Scotland, along with friends of missions among the Scottish Seceders, evangelical zeal tempering the keenness of ecclesiastical antagonism. Within a few years of the establishment of those two Societies, the Scottish Churches were virtually, although not formally, represented in the East Indies by a Bombay Mission, afterwards taken over (in 1835) by the Church of Scotland; in the West Indies by a Jamaica station, subsequently entrusted (in 1847) to the United Presbyterian Church; in Africa by a Kaffir Mission, eventually (in 1844) transferred to the Free Church.[20]

It is noteworthy, moreover, as an illustration of Scottish influence at this period in the growth of missionary enterprise, that a minister of the Church of Scotland, Dr. John Love, an early office-bearer of the Glasgow Association, had been one of the chief founders, as well as the first secretary of the London Missionary Society.[21] More notable still is the fact that, several years before William Carey arrived in Bengal, an eminent Scotsman, Charles Grant of Inverness-shire, afterwards Chairman of the East India Company, had paved the way for missionary progress, both by personal effort in India and by influence over friends at home. It was Charles Grant who, in 1786, maintained, at his own expense, the first British missionary —Thomas[22]—who laboured in Bengal. It was from Charles Grant that Carey received in 1793 his warmest and most influential welcome; and by his prudent counsel the new mission, when it failed to secure freedom for its operations in British India, was transferred to the Danish settlement of Serampore. It was through Charles Grant that Simeon of Cambridge, the leader of the English Evangelicals, devoted part of his strength to the Mission cause, and joined with Grant and others in founding the Church Missionary Society in 1799. Through the influence of Grant, mainly, the East India Company was gradually converted from its antagonistic attitude towards missions, and inaugurated the later policy of friendly toleration towards the propagators of Christian truth. A writing of his, composed in 1792, addressed to his East India co-Directors in 1797, and eventually published by order of the House of Commons,[23] was regarded at the time as the best counteractive to the sneers of Sydney Smith. It anticipated in outline the Indian educational reforms and missionary programme of the nineteenth century, and it had a chief share in the enlightenment of British public opinion. Finally, after his return from India, as M.P. for the county of Inverness from 1802, Grant was for about twenty years, in the House of Commons, the leading exponent and advocate of a thoroughly Christian Indian policy.[24]

IV. It will thus be seen that, both during the period when Reformed Christendom was culpably negligent of missionary duty, and also during the epoch, at the close of last century, when the missionary revival began, the Scottish Church and its representatives contributed substantially, and even signally, to the narrow yet gradually broadening stream of evangelistic enterprise. It is owing mainly, however, to the work of two eminent Scotsmen of later date that Scotland occupies a conspicuously influential place in the history of modern missions. These two are Alexander Duff and David Livingstone. Other Scottish missionaries, indeed, of the present century have stood in the front ranks of the Gospel army. Robert Morrison,[25] the founder of Protestant missions in China, and the translator of the Bible into Chinese; Robert Moffat,[26] the apostle of Bechuana, who civilised as well as Christianised the fierce Kaffirs, and vindicated the humanity of the despised Hottentots;

John Wilson,[27] the leading founder of the Bombay Scottish Mission, and, for nearly half a century, the influential promoter of Christian education and philanthropic enterprise in Western India; John Gibson Paton,[28] apostle of the New Hebrides, and friend of the cannibals in the Western Pacific; William Macfarlane,[29] evangelist of the Lepchas and Bhootias in N.E. India, to whom the increase of interest in the aborigines of our Indian Empire is largely due; Alexander Mackay,[30] of Uganda, the story of whose devoted life and labours has done much to foster the demand for the establishment there of a permanent British protectorate — all these, among others, representing five different branches of what may be called, in the wide sense, the Scottish Church,[31] have extended their influence as missionaries far beyond their own local sphere of labour and their own particular section of Christendom. The two names, however, which are here placed at the head of the roll of modern Scottish evangelists, deserve special commemoration on account of unique service to the Mission cause. Alexander Duff effected a revolution in the method and scope of Indian missions, besides helping signally to mould our Indian policy. David Livingstone opened up to missionary as well as to commercial enterprise the unexplored quarter of a continent, and attracted towards "Darkest Africa" the sympathy of the world.

V. Alexander Duff holds a high place among modern apostles, but he himself, as regards missionary ideas, was in no small degree moulded and inspired by another personality, less widely known beyond Scotland, but not less highly venerated for his "sanctified statesmanship" by the Scottish Church. John Inglis—the most sagacious divine of his day,[32] as his recently removed son was the most sagacious Scottish judge of his time—deserves commemoration, both because he was the founder of the earliest mission of the Scottish Church, as a Church, in modern times, and also because he was "the sole and undisputed author," to use Dr. Duff's generous words,[33] of the new missionary policy which the latter developed in detail and carried into successful operation. A powerful sermon preached by Dr. Inglis in 1818, in connection with the Society for the Propagation of Christian Knowledge; a memorable resolution of the General Assembly in 1824, unanimously adopted through his great personal influence as well as irresistible arguments; and an impressive Pastoral Letter, written by him in the name of the Church, and read to all her congregations, became the means of the Church of Scotland taking her place in the van of the missionary army.[34] Although Dr. Inglis had never visited India, he understood its missionary needs more clearly than many who had laboured there for nearly half a lifetime. In the true spirit of the Scottish Church, which had ever emphasised the teaching as well as the preaching of the truth, and the union of secular with religious instruction, he discerned that India required a great system of national education permeated with Christianity, and in particular a combined educational and missionary organisation. Thus only could the Christian faith be rooted firmly in the national mind, and a fully equipped class of native Christian teachers, preachers, and social leaders be reared—men whose minds would be stored with knowledge and invigorated by intellectual exercise; men qualified to be the religious guides of their fellow-countrymen, and capable alike of themselves giving, and of teaching others to give, a reason for the faith that was in them.

The history of religion in India had reached at this period a critical stage. For a full generation two fresh currents of influence had been affecting Hindoo faith. On the one hand, the missionary activity inaugurated by Schwarz, and continued by Carey [35] and others, had been operating with considerable result among the lower strata of Hindoo society, through vernacular preaching and schools, Scriptures and tracts. On the other hand, the influence of Western literature, philosophy, and science had begun to tell upon the upper social strata, particularly upon the high-caste Brahman population, and to loosen their faith in the religion of their forefathers. In 1817 there had been opened in Calcutta, under conjoined English and native auspices, a Hindoo College, at which Western higher education was communicated to the *élite* of the native youth. The issue was that, under the search-light of European science, the falsehood of the physics with which Hindoo theology was inextricably interwoven became patent to the educated native mind. Among cultured Hindoos, accordingly, the old faith was gone or going; and unfortunately, so far as they were concerned, nothing was taking its place. The favourite text-books at the Hindoo College were, in philosophy, Hume's *Essays* and Paine's *Age of Reason;* in literature, the licentious dramas of the Restoration age. While Christianity, after long repression, was beginning to reach and to impress the lower castes, influential Hindoo society was drifting rapidly into scepticism and secularism.[36]

At this grave crisis Alexander Duff arrived in India, with the educational ideas of Inglis in his head and the glow of missionary enthusiasm in his heart. He had not been long in Calcutta when he discerned the wisdom of the policy whose general outline had been sketched for him, but whose details were left to himself to supply. "The few converts that have been made in India," he wrote, "can never be the seed of the Church : they resemble rather those short-lived germs which start up under the influence of a few genial days in winter; let us reach forward to the full life and verdure of spring, when the whole earth shall be loosened from its torpour." Changing the figure, he likens the work hitherto accomplished to the separation of precious atoms from the mass of the heathen rock. What was needed, he said, and what the Scottish Mission aimed at effecting, was the "setting of a train which shall one day explode and tear up the whole from its lower depths." [37]

The Scottish scheme of Christian education combined with Western culture had been partially anticipated a few years before. In 1818 Carey had established at Serampore an institution for the "instruction of Asiatic youth," not only in "Eastern literature" but in "European science"; and in 1820 Bishop Middleton had to some extent followed his example by founding "Bishop's College," three miles out of Calcutta. But neither institution fully met the special need of the time. Carey's College was broad in its scope, but its development had been arrested by inadequacy of material support; [38] Middleton's was amply endowed, but it aimed too narrowly at rearing a native ministry to work under episcopal jurisdiction; [39] while both institutions laboured under the fatal drawback of not being in Calcutta itself, and therefore of not meeting the sceptical and secularistic influence of the Hindoo College on its own arena. Duff discerned the causes of comparative failure, and determined to establish, under the very shadow of the pagan institute, a fully equipped and catholic Christian rival.

In the missionary circles, as a whole, of Bengal his scheme met with disfavour. Educational work, indeed, under missionary auspices, was approved. Through vernacular schools it was already carried on in Calcutta and elsewhere. But higher education, communicated through the English tongue, and embracing Western science and culture along with Christian knowledge, was generally regarded as useless, if not pernicious. High-caste Brahmans, it was argued, would not come in any number to a college where they must listen to Christian as well as to secular teaching, and the few who came would drink in infidelity at the secular fountains, without imbibing Christianity at the religious well.[40] From Carey almost alone Duff received encouragement to proceed, but Carey's sympathy was worth the approval of a thousand. Few scenes in missionary history are more touching than the first interview between the veteran apostle, already tottering on the brink of the grave, and the young recruit who had come to carry out more fully, and under more favourable auspices, the work which the other had partially attempted. Without one thought of ignoble envy, and in the spirit of Moses strengthening Joshua on the eve of the conquest from which he himself was debarred, the aged missionary leader bestowed on the young Scotsman and the Scottish enterprise his warm benediction, unselfishly rejoicing in the prospective triumph under another which he had once hoped himself to attain.[41]

Like all great pioneers, Duff found that he must "stoop to conquer." Students would not leave the Hindoo College for his missionary institute; he had to make his bricks as well as to build his house. He began by teaching the very elements of English to native scholars, and after years of drudgery the human material was prepared for the higher Christian education which it was his special aim to impart.[42] He had to encounter, also, not only the warnings of fellow-missionaries, but the opposition of Orientalists, as they were called, who decried all culture for Hindoos except on Oriental lines;[43] the hostility, moreover, of orthodox natives who raised the cry of Hindooism in danger.[44] But he persevered, and by and by he began to reap a substantial harvest. The capacity of his trained scholars for grasping Christian truth astonished educational inquirers.[45] Out of those who received Christian facts and doctrines into their heads, a fair proportion received Christianity into their hearts, braved the domestic or social excommunication which Christian profession entailed, and became influential witnesses on the side of Christian faith.[46]

The successful example of Dr. Duff led to a new departure, alike in Indian missionary operations and in Indian educational policy. In the missionary sphere, the majority of the leading Societies—even of those farthest removed, ecclesiastically, from the Church of Scotland—gradually adopted, more or less, the Scottish method, not, of course, to the exclusion of vernacular teaching and preaching, but as an indispensable department of a complete missionary organisation.[47] In the educational sphere, the Indian Government, which had hitherto encouraged native culture only on Oriental lines, now gave to English studies a prominent place in the academic curriculum, and aimed at putting the young Brahmans of Calcutta, as regards Western learning and science, on a level with the youth of Oxford or Edinburgh.[48] "It was the special glory of Alexander Duff"—so the Bishop of Calcutta, Dr. Cotton, testified in 1863—"that, arriving here in the midst of a great intellectual awakening of atheistical character, he resolved to make that character Christian. When the new generation of Bengalees were talking of Christianity as an obsolete superstition, soon to be burnt up on the pyre on which the creeds of Brahman, Buddhist, and Mahometan were already perishing, Alexander Duff burst on the scene with his unhesitating faith, indomitable courage, varied erudition, and never-failing stream of fervid eloquence, to teach them that the Gospel was neither ashamed nor unable to vindicate its claims to universal reverence, but was marching forward in the van of civilisation."[49] To select one other witness from a different section of Anglo-Indian influential society, Sir Charles Trevelyan, who held high office in the East India Company, testifies warmly to the "important influence of Dr. Duff's exertions upon the action of the Government"; to the "direct access gained to the future leaders of the people" through the Calcutta College and similar institutions established after its pattern; to the "new respect paid to missionaries as tutors of young native chiefs and other highly considered persons" who attended the mission colleges; and to Dr. Duff's "sagacity at this crisis of Indian history" in distinguishing between "the present abuse" of Western learning and "the important use to which, under proper direction, it might be applied in aid of the Christian cause. These were great and pregnant reforms, which must always give Dr. Duff a high place among the benefactors of mankind."[50]

VI. More than sixty years have passed since the missionary method designed by Inglis and inaugurated by Duff was applied to the soil of Indian heathendom, and if the spiritual harvest has not been so abundant and so speedy as was at first expected, these results have been attained :

1. Through those numerous Christian colleges and schools which owe their existence largely to Dr. Duff's successful example, a Christian atmosphere has been created which makes the profession of Christianity conspicuously less difficult for the converted native, and renders all missionary agencies correspondingly more productive of visible results.

2. Through the introduction of Western ideas and culture into Hindoo higher education, the foundation was laid for that great ally of evangelistic preaching and Christian education, the Medical Mission, which owed to Scottish enterprise its earliest separate organisation.[51] The desire also of natives, especially Hindoos of higher caste, for the education of their women has been fostered, and the long-closed door has thus been opened for what many regard as the chief factor of Indian evangelisation—female Christian education.

3. The value of the Scottish missionary policy must be measured not only by the good accomplished, but by the evil prevented; and it was the timely establishment of Christian colleges by the Scottish missionaries and their imitators which saved Hindoo culture from becoming not only, as now, largely, but almost wholly, secular and infidel.

4. We must reckon not only results achieved in the past, but prospects opened up in the future. The belief that India, as a whole, will be won for Christianity rests chiefly, under God, on the hoped-for rise of a succession of native Christian apostles (seconded by an efficient native ministry), through whom the millions of the vast population will be turned to Christ by the magnetic power which only a fellow-countryman can widely exert. For such apostolates the mission colleges are preparing the way, by causing Christian knowledge to permeate the influential sections of Indian society.

After the experience, accordingly, of over half a century, it is recognised by the great majority of competent witnesses that Christian institutions for native higher education, through the English language, are an indispensable and eminently effective instrument of missionary success and of moral and spiritual progress.⁵² The verdict of British governors and commissioners, missionaries and clergy, outstanding civilians and military officers, is confirmed by the testimony of non-Christian native opinion. A leader of the theistic Brahmo Somaj publicly declared, a few years ago, that he knew the students of mission colleges by their having "more backbone and moral principle"; while an influential organ of the anti-Christian Arya Somaj candidly admits that the higher "educational department has most markedly contributed to swell the ranks of converts," and that with it "is associated the memory of the missionaries' most splendid achievements in proselytisation." ⁵³

VII. David Livingstone entered on his missionary career in 1840 under the auspices of the London Missionary Society, whose headquarters are in that city, but whose supporters include the membership of at least one Christian denomination in Scotland.⁵⁴ The Scottish Church, in the broad sense, claims him not only as a son, but as a characteristic representative. His father and forefathers belonged to "Ulva's Isle," close to the cradle of Scottish Christianity. His mother was a descendant of sturdy Covenanters. He was reared in connection with the "Kirk of Scotland," which he continued to recognise, after he became a Congregationalist, as a "religious establishment which has been an incalculable blessing to that country."[55] He grew up in a home where, as he himself relates, the old-fashioned ideal of Scottish piety "so beautifully portrayed in the 'Cottar's Saturday Night'" was realised, and in a county rich in those traditions of persecuted Presbyterianism whose hallowing influence he loved in later days to recall.[56] In the records of his life there are frequent indications that the friend of Africa and the citizen of the world never ceased to be a patriotic Scot.[57]

As Alexander Duff created a new era in Indian missions by the union of evangelistic effort with the communication of Western culture, so David Livingstone inaugurated a fresh epoch in African evangelisation by associating missionary enterprise with geographical exploration. There were great African missionaries and distinguished African explorers before his time; he was great in both spheres. He left the service of the London Society in order not to be hampered in his expeditions by the ideas of narrow-minded friends of missions;[58] he declined to be the salaried servant of the Geographical Society, lest his missionary aims should be affected by his obligations as a professional explorer.[59] But in his eyes exploration was ever the means, evangelisation the end. The love of travel was subordinated to the love of Christ, and consecrated to the service of mankind.

Livingstone's influence in rousing Christendom to missionary and philanthropic, as well as geographical and commercial, interest in Africa is universally recognised. He revolutionised men's ideas both as to that continent and as to its population. He proved that its central and unexplored regions were not vast deserts but fruitful and comparatively healthy lands, in which colonists and missionaries (under suitable furlough arrangements) could live and work. He taught the Church that the populations of those newly explored territories were men and women not without amiable features of character, capable of instruction, susceptible of civilisation, and hopeful subjects of missionary effort. He set before Europe and America, with a fulness of detail and an earnestness of purpose exhibited by no preceding explorer, the infamous horrors of the African slave-traffic; and he revived, as well as directed into a definite channel, the anti-slavery zeal of Christendom. Above all, he presented to the world the bright and stimulating example of single-minded and enthusiastic devotion to the welfare of the "Dark Continent," so that multitudes were interested in Africa and its people through first learning to love and revere Livingstone, Africa's friend. Hence resulted the unique impulse given by him to African missionary enterprise. Not a Missionary Society of any importance in Britain or America failed to be moved by Livingstone's appeal, addressed immediately to the students of Cambridge, but intended for the Christian world: "Africa is now open: do not let it be shut again. The work which I have begun.

I leave with you."[60] His whole life was a missionary incentive. His pathetic death was a philanthropic inspiration. His influence furnished Africa with a regiment of evangelists, and whetted the sword from which the African slave-trade has received, if not its immediate death, at least its mortal wound.

This was not all. In another aspect, not less important, but less generally recognised, Livingstone created a new era in African evangelisation. He not only sent missionaries to Africa, he prepared Africa for the missionary. Pre-eminently beyond all previous explorers, even the most philanthropic, Livingstone succeeded in convincing the negro that the white man was his friend, and that the white man's religion was a blessed reality. Ever gentle and tenderly considerate in his dealings with native populations, he traversed their territory, and made them feel that he traversed it, not as a mere scientific inquirer, but as a sympathetic brother; and he won their grateful confidence and affectionate reverence. The familiar story of his last illness and his death on the shore of Lake Bangweolo; the devoted ministry of his faithful African attendants to the dying hero; their grief on the morning when they found him dead, in the posture of prayer; their rough but effective embalming of his body; their heroic resolution, inflexibly carried out, to convey his remains and belongings to Zanzibar, over a thousand miles of territory, through hostile as well as friendly populations, in order that he might be taken home thence for burial by his nearest and dearest—all this constitutes a signal chapter in the modern history of Africa, for it proved that the white man had won the black man's heart.[61] To this day the name of Livingstone—the "Great Master," as he is reverently called—is a word of power in Central Africa, and his memory is a precious treasure, cherished as that of a superior being. The good feeling and trustfulness of the native races as a whole towards Britain, in what is now the British Protectorate, and the religious receptiveness of the peoples now being evangelised by English, Scottish, and American Missions, are largely due, directly or indirectly, to the influence of Livingstone's memory, and to the belief that the missionaries who seek their welfare are Livingstone's friends.[62]

Those whose position and experience give them a claim to be heard are persuaded that a great future is in store for Central Africa, and especially for the British territory there, at once as an imperial colony and as a province of Christendom; and no future historian of the continent will fail to recall how, under Providence, the way was mainly prepared, both here and there, for that promised issue by the great Scottish missionary who opened the heart of Christendom for Africa and the heart of the African for Christianity.

LECTURE III

THE INFLUENCE OF THE SCOTTISH REFORMED
CHURCH IN ENGLAND AND IN IRELAND

AT the period of the Reformation close relations subsisted between England and Scotland through royal affinity, political confederacy, and the provision of a refuge, at different junctures, by each country for the Protestant exiles from the other.[1] It was inevitable, accordingly, that the Reformed Churches of the two nations should exert some influence over each other's external fortunes and internal development. Particularly notable is the influence at that epoch, as well as afterward, of the smaller Scottish Church over the greater Church of England.

I. From the return of Mary Stewart to Scotland in the autumn of 1561 to her flight into England in the summer of 1568, British

Protestantism was in constant peril; and even when the fugitive Queen had become a prisoner at Fotheringay, the danger was far from being removed. Mary came to Scotland with the double ambition of restoring Romanism throughout Britain and of becoming eventually Queen of England as well as of her own realm; she refused either to acknowledge formally the Scottish Reformation or to renounce her claim to the English crown.[2] During the first four years of her personal rule the Queen's influence increased, while that of the Protestant statesmen of Scotland declined; her triumph culminated at the time of her marriage with Darnley, when the Earl of Moray and other nobles who had risen in rebellion were driven across the Border into exile. In England at this period, especially in the north, where Catholics were numerous and influential, there was a strong party of conspirators against Protestantism, whose aim was either to dethrone Elizabeth and enthrone Mary, or to force upon the former the restoration of the Catholic Church.[3] Throughout both England and Scotland, moreover, the Jesuits were beginning to exert that marvellous faculty of political and ecclesiastical intrigue for which they became notorious in Christendom.[4] On the Continent, prior to Mary's return to Scotland, a great Catholic League had been projected for the extirpation of Protestantism; and the overthrow of the Reformed English Church was, in particular, the object of manifold intrigue. If the Queen of Scots, after her return, did not formally join this League, she was, at least, in frequent correspondence with her relatives in France, with the King of Spain, and with the Pope, regarding the restoration of Roman Catholicism throughout Britain.[5] What prevented the success of the manifold and constant plots against English Protestantism? The causes of failure were various, and included mutual jealousies among Catholic potentates and parties. But not least among the forces which at this critical period saved the Reformed Church of England from peril were the staunch Protestantism, enlightened patriotism, and statesmanlike vigilance of the leaders of the Scottish Church. To the influence of the Scottish Reformed Church it was largely due that no foreign invasion of England by way of Scotland could be accomplished, and that no effective combination between Scottish and English Catholics was practicable. To the religious patriotism of Knox and his associates it was owing that grave internal differences between the Protestant nobility and the Reformed clergy, regarding the Church's patrimony and organisation, did not (ultimately at least) prevent the combination of the two parties against common foes. Through the same influence, Scottish Protestantism was neither alienated by the duplicity of Elizabeth, nor seduced by the fascinations of Mary, from that friendly co-operation with the English Government which, at this juncture, was the indispensable condition of England, even more than it was of Scotland, being conserved as part of Reformed Christendom.[6]

II. The influence of the Reformed Scottish Church was not less upon the internal development than upon the external fortunes of English Protestantism. The main difference between the English and the Scottish Reformation is well known. The former, more conservative in character, was guided and controlled by leaders whose aim was the establishment of a Church independent of Rome, and purged from Romish error and corruption, yet with the minimum of divergence from the Roman Catholic Church as regarded ritual, organisation, and religious usage. The Scottish Reformation was more radical in character. It was directed and moulded by men who considered less the continuity than the purity of the Church, and who emphasised, as the rule alike of faith, worship, and Church government, not ecclesiastical tradition, however venerable, but simply and solely the Word of God.

From the outset, however, many Protestants in England had greater sympathy with the Scottish than with the English ideal and method of reformation. On this party, and through it on the Church of England as a whole, the influence of the Scottish Church was most considerable; and that influence was exerted both before and after divergence of view among English Protestants deepened, on the one side, into Anglican intolerance, on the other, into Puritan secession. In the latter part of the reign of Henry VIII., several outstanding Scotsmen of reforming views—including three notable Dominicans, Alexander Seton, John M'Alpine, and John M'Dowel [7]—were driven by persecution into exile, and occupied positions of influence in the English Church. More conspicuously, during the reign of Edward VI. (1547 - 53), when the persecution of Protestants still prevailed in Scotland, England became a refuge for Scottish Reforming leaders and preachers. At a time when the majority of bishops, lower clergy, and people were still opposed to change either in creed or in ritual, John Knox, John Rough, John Willock, John M'Brair, and other Scotsmen exercised their gifts south of the Tweed, with the special sanction of the English Government.[8]

John Knox in particular exerted, at this period, on the partially Reformed Church of England a considerable portion of that directing and controlling influence which, from first to last, belonged to his well-defined views, powerful oratory, and impressive personality. So great was the effect of his preaching at this juncture that English papists, as Mary Stewart afterwards told him, ascribed his power to infernal agency.[9] At Berwick, where a laborious ministry of two years was the means of winning to the Reformed Faith a large proportion of the citizenship, and of visibly amending the morale of the garrison;[10] at Newcastle, where he had the opportunity of expounding his views on the Mass before the "Council of the North,"[11] and where his signal success, along with the desire to get rid of too plain-spoken a preacher, moved the Duke of Northumberland to offer him the See of Rochester;[12] in London, where he held the high office of a Royal Chaplain,[13] with the double duty of preaching before the Court and itinerating on behalf of the Reform cause —in all these positions Knox was influential in the establishment of Protestantism, and pre-eminent in the propagation of what afterwards came to be known as Puritanism. He was the first notable ecclesiastic who introduced into England what was then the startling innovation of sitting instead of kneeling at the Holy Communion, in order to avoid the danger of the idolatry of the Host. This innovation, in great measure through his example and advocacy, ere long became common, and constitutes the inauguration of

Puritan, as distinguished from High Anglican worship.[14] It was mainly, also, through the influence of Knox, as Royal Chaplain, with the Privy Council, that what extreme High Churchmen call the "Black Rubric," but what Anglicans with Protestant sympathies regard as a bulwark of vital truth, was inserted into the Revised Prayer-Book of 1552 at the end of the Communion office. This notable rubric—deleted, after Elizabeth's accession, to propitiate Catholics, replaced at the Restoration to conciliate Puritans, and still retained— declares distinctly that by the posture of kneeling "no adoration is intended" either of the sacramental bread and wine ("for that were idolatry") or of "Christ's natural Flesh and Blood," which "are in heaven and not here."[15] To Knox, moreover, and to his influence, direct and indirect, at this formative period of the Anglican Church, may be ascribed, in some measure, the character and mould of the "Forty-two Articles" which afterwards became the "Thirty-nine." These articles, the composition mainly of Cranmer— were submitted to the Royal Chaplains in draft. There is evidence of one notable alteration having been made in consequence of objections taken by John Knox and some of his colleagues. We may reasonably conclude, in the light of his position at Court, as well as of his relations with Cranmer and other English Church dignitaries, that he was more or less consulted in the framing of a Confession with which his own views were in substantial accord.[16]

During the reign of Mary Tudor (1553-58) the influence of Knox on the English Church continued to be exerted, although mainly on a different arena. For seven months after Mary's accession he remained in England at the peril of his life; and we find him preaching laboriously in London, Carlisle, and Kent, after almost every other Protestant voice had been silenced by royal interdict.[17] During his exile on the Continent, numerous writings from his prolific pen—"comfortable epistles" and "faithful admonitions"—helped to sustain under trial the faith of his personal friends and former congregations in England.[18] Of the English refugees during the Marian persecution—estimated at fully a thousand—a large proportion formed themselves into

Puritan, as distinguished from High Anglican, worship.[14] It was mainly, also, through the influence of Knox, as Royal Chaplain, with the Privy Council, that what extreme High Churchmen call the "Black Rubric," but what Anglicans with Protestant sympathies regard as a bulwark of vital truth, was inserted into the Revised Prayer-Book of 1552 at the end of the Communion office. This notable rubric—deleted, after Elizabeth's accession, to propitiate Catholics, replaced at the Restoration to conciliate Puritans, and still retained—declares distinctly that by the posture of kneeling "no adoration is intended" either of the sacramental bread and wine ("for that were idolatry") or of "Christ's natural Flesh and Blood," which "are in heaven and not here."[15] To Knox, moreover, and to his influence, direct and indirect, at this formative period of the Anglican Church, may be ascribed, in some measure, the character and mould of the "Forty-two Articles" which afterwards became the "Thirty-nine." These articles, the composition mainly of Cranmer—were submitted to the Royal Chaplains in draft. There is evidence of one notable alteration having been made in consequence of objections taken by John Knox and some of his colleagues. We may reasonably conclude, in the light of his position at Court, as well as of his relations with Cranmer and other English Church dignitaries, that he was more or less consulted in the framing of a Confession with which his own views were in substantial accord.[16]

During the reign of Mary Tudor (1553-58) the influence of Knox on the English Church continued to be exerted, although mainly on a different arena. For seven months after Mary's accession he remained in England at the peril of his life; and we find him preaching laboriously in London, Carlisle, and Kent, after almost every other Protestant voice had been silenced by royal interdict.[17] During his exile on the Continent, numerous writings from his prolific pen—"comfortable epistles" and "faithful admonitions"—helped to sustain under trial the faith of his personal friends and former congregations in England.[18] Of the English refugees during the Marian persecution—estimated at fully a thousand—a large proportion formed themselves into congregations at Frankfort and at Geneva; and the influential position held among them by Knox is attested by his appointment as pastor, in each of these cities successively, over congregations which included such notable English divines as Whittingham, Gilby, Foxe, Cole, Coverdale, and Sampson.[19] The congregation at Geneva, numbering over two hundred members, was decidedly Puritan in character; and, on the accession of Elizabeth, when it became expedient to issue a Puritan manifesto in view of a fresh ecclesiastical settlement, it was upon Knox that the task devolved. His *Brief Exhortation to England*,[20] as the treatise was called, advocating substantially such a modification of episcopacy and such a system of national education as he afterwards established in Scotland, constitutes the earliest definite programme of the more radical English Reformers. It justifies Carlyle's designation of Knox as the "chief priest and founder" of English Puritanism.[21]

III. The accomplishment of the Reformation in Scotland on Calvinistic lines, in 1560, could not fail to encourage the English Puritans in their efforts to secure for their views toleration and eventual ascendency. The Scottish General Assembly of 1566 sent a letter to the clergy of the sister Church, pleading for Christian charity and consideration towards those Puritan ministers who were unable, in the matter of vestments, to conform to ecclesiastical usage.[22] When a division took place, at this juncture, in the Puritan ranks, Scottish influence over English Churchmen was manifested, both in the case of the seceding minority and in that of the remanent majority. The former maintained in secret a Presbyterian organisation, as well as an order of worship according to Knox's *Book of Geneva*; the latter were encouraged by Scottish example and counsel to fight the battle of Puritanism and Presbyterianism within, instead of outside, the National Church. Scottish ecclesiastical institutions and usages began to be reproduced in England. The weekly "Exercise" or "Prophesying," which formed part of the early organisation of the Reformed Church of Scotland, and out of which the Presbytery afterwards developed, was instituted at Northampton in 1571, and subsequently became common in the English

Church. In 1572, the foundation of English Presbyterianism was laid by the constitution of a "Presbytery" or Kirk-Session at Wandsworth, near London. The English *Book of Discipline*, published in 1583, and signed by 500 clergy of the Church of England,—the "Palladium of English Presbyterianism"— was partly modelled on the Scottish *Book of Discipline*, composed twenty years before by Knox and his colleagues. While these ecclesiastical developments were not peculiar to Scotland, the influence of the Scottish Church in leading to their reproduction in England is amply attested by the significant charge of "Scottizing" brought by Dr. Bancroft, afterwards Primate of England, against the Puritan party in his own Church.[23]

On the accession of James VI. in 1603 to the English throne, the known sympathy of the Scottish Church and the supposed sympathy of the Scottish King encouraged the English Puritans to seek, through the famous Millenary and other petitions, the removal of grievances and the reformation of usages which were estranging them from the Church of England.[24] The petitions were disregarded; but at once their presentation and their rejection contributed to the consolidation of the Puritan party. In the succeeding reign of Charles I., the inauguration of Puritan and Presbyterian resistance to the Romanising policy of Laud was due to a Scottish minister in London, Dr. Alexander Leighton, the father of the future Archbishop of Glasgow. Leighton's *Plea against the Prelacy* received the signed approval of 500 notable persons in England; and the brutal punishment of branding and mutilation which he endured contributed materially to the antiprelatical movement in the English Church, by enlisting the sympathy of thousands who had never read a line of his book.[25] A few years later, the triumph of the National Covenant in Scotland, the displacement of Scottish Episcopacy and replacement of Presbyterianism in 1638, the extensive circulation in England of controversial pamphlets by Alexander Henderson and other prominent Covenanters, along with their personal influence and pulpit eloquence during protracted negotiations in England with Charles I. in 1640—all combined to stimulate powerfully the movement which issued in the overthrow of English Episcopacy by the Long Parliament (1642) and in the convocation of the Westminster Assembly for the settlement, on a fresh basis, of the Church's doctrine, worship, and government.[26] When Parliament, in the following year, followed up that procedure by the establishment of Presbyterianism, this momentous step was initiated with the signature of a manifesto drawn up by Scottish Churchmen and previously approved by the Scottish General Assembly—the memorable Solemn League and Covenant. Not without significance, on the day (15th of September 1643) when the members of the Long Parliament and of the Westminster Assembly —the representatives of Church and State— stood up together in the Church of St. Margaret at Westminster with right hands raised to heaven, and took a solemn oath of fidelity to the Covenant, one of the two addresses was delivered by the Scottish Church leader, Alexander Henderson. In the other, Philip Nye, the English Independent, referred pointedly to the "light and beauty in matters of order and discipline manifested by the churches of Scotland"; while, in all the sermons delivered on the occasion, the attitude of the

Scottish Covenanters was prominently referred to as a motive to the adoption of the Covenant by the English nation. The Westminster Assembly, in its exhortation to the people of England, dwells upon the fact that the "whole body of Scotland had willingly sworn and subscribed" the Covenant, and that God had "vouchsafed to disperse and scatter those dark clouds which overshadowed that loyal and religious kingdom" after "they had entered into such a solemn League and Covenant at the beginning of the late troubles there."[27]

IV. The Presbyterian ascendency in England, superficial and shortlived as it was, derived the greater part of such strength and prestige as it possessed from the more thorough and deep-rooted Presbyterianism of the sister kingdom; and when the day of reaction came, after the restoration of the monarchy, it was to Scottish influence, in part at least, that the preservation of English Presbyterianism was due. The ejection of 2000 English Presbyterian ministers from their parishes in 1662 by the Act of Uniformity, without any provision being made for their maintenance, and the breaking up of their congregations by the

Conventicle and Five Mile Acts, reduced the Presbyterianism of England to a feeble remnant. That it was not utterly extinguished, and that the ousted English pastors, with their congregations, maintained, amid repressive statutes and social traducement, some organised existence, was due, in part, to the example of heroic endurance shown by the Scottish Covenanters in a still hotter furnace of persecution. Alexander Peden, from whom a hill near Otterburn in Northumberland, on which he was wont to preach, has received its name; William Veitch, who spent many years of his life in the same county, as well as in London and other parts of England; and Alexander Carmichael, who, after his exile in 1672, became minister of a Presbyterian congregation in London, are prominent examples, among many, of Scottish Covenanters during the "killing times," who found in England at once a comparatively safe refuge and a sphere of zealous and influential ministry.[28]

In the eighteenth century, English Presbyterianism, delivered by the Revolution of 1688 from external trouble, was subjected to the yet worse evil of internal declension; and the

Westminster Creed was depreciated and even discarded by Arian or Socinian successors of the Westminster divines.[29] Scotland itself was at this period by no means free from the same taint;[30] yet through Scottish influence, mainly, an orthodox and evangelical element was conserved in the Presbyterian Church of England. In London and elsewhere, especially after the Union of the Kingdoms in 1707, congregations composed mainly of Scotsmen or their descendants, and ministered to by Scottish pastors, became rallying centres of evangelical Presbyterianism amid prevalent decadence. Testimony is borne in 1772 that the "Scots' Presbytery" in London, in spite of the taunt that they were "not dissenters upon principles of liberty," had "inviolably maintained the faith and spirit of the parent church (of Scotland) in the land where Providence had cast their lot."[31] The main strongholds, however, of English Presbyterian fidelity to vital truth, during this century of theological down-grade, were in the northern counties. The ecclesiastical intercourse of Presbyterians there with the Church of Scotland was particularly frequent;[32] and the ministers were mostly men who had been trained for the pastorate in Scottish Universities. The anti-Arian influence thus exerted by Scottish upon English Presbyterianism may be estimated from the significant complaint, made in 1737 by a Yorkshire Presbyterian minister of Arian views, that "in Northumberland, Cumberland, and some other places," every vacancy was "attempted to be supplied from Scotland." This practice he declares to be "a fatal obstacle to the removal of attachment to confessions of faith."[33]

Finally, the revival of English Presbyterianism, as a whole, on evangelical lines, in the early part of the present century, was due, in great measure, to the previous revival of religion both in the National Church of Scotland and in the Secession Churches. The wave of Scottish spiritual life, which gathered volume through the ministry of Chalmers in Glasgow and of Andrew Thomson in Edinburgh, overflowed into England. Earnest Scotsmen, both pastors and laymen, who crossed the Border, communicated the new life and religious zeal of which they had themselves become possessed. Numerous English Presbyterian congregations formed themselves into a Synod which, although not subject to Scottish ecclesiastical jurisdiction, was in close communion with the Church of Scotland and largely under its influence. After the appointment of Chalmers to the Chair of Theology in Edinburgh (1828), English as well as Scottish students crowded his lecture-room, came under the spell of his fervid teaching, and bore away from the northern capital, to their varied spheres of pastoral labour, seeds of spiritual vitality and energy which fructified in every corner of England.[34]

V. Not the Presbyterianism only of England has been influenced by Scotland during the period subsequent to the Revolution ; nor through the dominant Presbyterian Scottish Church alone has the religious and ecclesiastical influence of Scotland upon England been exerted. The Church of Scotland owes a deep debt of gratitude to the learning of her English sister, whose ampler endowments have enabled her to cultivate more extensively many fields of historical research and theological inquiry ; but eminent representatives of the Church of England have acknowledged that the Church of Campbell, Beattie, and Reid in the eighteenth century, and of Chalmers, Macleod, Macleod Campbell, Tulloch, Milligan, and Robertson Smith (not to mention living divines) in the nineteenth, has repaid the debt in several important spheres of religious thought.[35] From the Scottish Church, moreover, the Church of England has received, in the century now closing, not a few of her eminent dignitaries and divines, including a recent Archbishop of Canterbury, and the present Archbishop of York.

In recent days the Scottish Episcopal Church has been potently affected by the Church of England, whose liturgy it uses, whose clergy it extensively imports, and whose varied tendencies and developments it reflects and reproduces. But the Church of England, in times not very remote, was considerably influenced by the Episcopal Church of Scotland. In the end of the last, and in the beginning of the present, century, long prior to the Anglo-Catholic revival in England, the Scottish Episcopal clergy—notably Bishop John Skinner of Aberdeen, and Bishop Jolly of Moray and Ross—set a conspicuous example of devotion to those patristic studies which afterwards caused a large and increasing section of the English Church to emphasise her Catholicity rather than her Protestantism.[36] The proximity, moreover, of a sister Episcopal Church, whose clergy for a whole century after the Revolution were non-jurors, could not but help to foster the anti-Erastianism which characterises the modern as distinguished from the earlier school of High Church Anglican divines. Similarly, the consecration of the first North American Bishop, Seabury, by the Scottish Episcopate in 1784, after English prelates had refused his application, led to the revisal in 1787, by the Church of England, of her pusillanimously Erastian policy.[37] Scottish bishops, also, owing to the declinature of the English hierarchy, consecrated at Stirling, in 1825, the first bishop set apart for the Episcopal superintendence of Anglican clergy and congregations on the Continent; and the enterprise of a Presbyter of the Scottish Episcopal Church—Dr. (afterwards Bishop) Walker, of Edinburgh,—inaugurated, eight years earlier, the Anglican service for British residents in Rome.[38] Finally, the synodical form of Church government exemplified by the Scottish Episcopal Church, along doubtless with the example of the Presbyterian General Assembly, helped to cause the revival, about the middle of this century, of the English House of Convocation.[39]

VI. English Methodism, in the latter part of the eighteenth century, influenced the Churches of Scotland more than it was influenced by them; although John Wesley once complained bitterly of the "dead unfeeling multitudes of Scotland," whom he contrasted with the "living stones" of the northern English counties.[40] Yet Methodism received as well as gave; it drew preachers from, as well as gave them to, Scotland. While in many respects, moreover, the Church of the Wesleys differs from Presbyterianism both in doctrine and in discipline, there can be no doubt that in the transformation of Methodism, towards the close of the eighteenth century, from a Society within the Church of England into an organisation outside of it, the neighbourhood of a national Presbyterian Church in Scotland exercised an appreciable influence both as an incentive and as a model. "As soon as I am dead," said Wesley, "the Methodists will be a regular Presbyterian Church."[41] His own maternal grandfather and great grandfather had been notable Presbyterians; his father had been educated as a Presbyterian student;[42] and he himself, in his system, adopted that compromise between Episcopacy and Presbytery which in the Scottish Reformed Church had been originally instituted but afterwards discarded —the office of the Superintendent, above the ordinary pastors as individuals, but subject to their jurisdiction as a body. In 1792, the Wesleyan leader Samuel Bradburn—the Methodist Demosthenes, as he has been called —frankly declared in a controversial tract, "Our Quarterly meetings answer to those Church meetings in Scotland called the Presbytery; our District meetings agree exactly with the Synod; and the Conference with the National or General Assembly." "Whatever we may choose to call ourselves, we must be Presbyterians."[43] A few years later, in 1796, a movement originated among the Methodists in favour of an equal proportion of pastors and laymen in the General Conference, after the model of the Scottish Church Courts; and it is significant that the leader of this new departure, Alexander Kilham, had laboured for three years as a superintendent in Scotland.[44] The movement, although defeated, was strong enough to result in the secession of 3000 members, who founded the New Connexion, now numbering 30,000; and, within recent years, the main body of Methodists have substantially adopted the views of the seceders by the establishment of a Representative Conference (auxiliary to the Conference proper), which takes place prior to that of pastors and superintendents, and in which ministers and lay-deputies sit together. The approach of Methodism to Presbyterianism has thus become another stage closer than before.

We have thus seen how, in each period of history since the Reformation, the influence of the Scottish on the English Church—in the wider sense of both words—has been always appreciable and often conspicuous. Scottish Protestantism helped to mould the doctrine and worship of the Reformed Church of England during the latter's infancy; it contributed afterwards to the growth of the revolt against her intolerance at more than one period of her maturity; it had some share, further, through varied channels of influence, in shaping the development both of the Church of England and of her great Methodist rival in modern times. Amid repeated fluctuations in the fortunes of English Presbyterianism, amid its external depression and its internal decadence, the Scottish Presbyterian Church has remained always a power—sometimes oppressed, sometimes dominant, now fervent, now moderate, here accepting, there renouncing State connection, but ever exerting an influence over its English Presbyterian sister by its sympathy, its activity, and, above all, its testimony.

From the influence of the Reformed Scottish Church in England we turn to the yet more signal part which it has taken in moulding the religious condition and ecclesiastical history of Ireland.

I. The early religious annals of Scotland and Ireland contain a notable record of mutual helpfulness. In the early part of the fifth century, while North Britain gave to the Irish their apostle and patron saint, Patrick of

Strathclyde, to Ireland North Britain appears to owe the conversion of Ternan, the evangelist of what is now Kincardineshire.[45] Towards the close of the same century, and in the early part of the sixth, eminent Irish saints, including Finnian of Moville, the teacher of Columba, received, as youths, their monastic and missionary training within the far-famed "Candida Casa" of Galloway;[46] and there is some evidence that, about the same time, Irish Christians were not only following with the Gospel message their fellow countrymen who had emigrated to North Britain, but were continuing the evangelisation, begun by St. Ninian, of the Southern Picts.[47] In the latter part of the sixth century, as was formerly noted, Ireland not only gave Columba to Scotland, but received in return from Iona part of that great missionary impulse which, during the seventh century, caused Irish monks to be the chief evangelists of Continental heathendom. In the former part of the eighth century, there came over from Ireland to Lochleven and elsewhere the original Culdees of Scotland, whose successors ministered to a large portion of the people, at first faithfully, afterwards negligently, down to the age of Queen Margaret.[48] This last spiritual benefaction remained for long substantially unrequited. At length, after an interval of nearly nine hundred years, it was abundantly repaid in that great movement of colonial propagation through which the Scottish Church in the seventeenth century became the mother of Irish Presbyterianism, and a bulwark of Irish Protestantism. If in the province of Ulster the Reformed Faith is conspicuously in the ascendant, although in Ireland, as a whole, the Roman Church claims three-fourths of the population; and if the enlightenment, enterprise, and prosperity of the North of Ireland equal those of any other portion of the British dominions, while the rest of the island, a few important centres and districts excepted, lags notably behind; this result is largely due to the Ulster Presbyterians, the descendants of Scottish settlers, who brought along with them, propagated around them, and transmitted to their posterity the doctrine, discipline, worship, and, above all, the spirit of the Reformed Scottish Church.[49]

II. Three memorable events in the seventeenth century led to the exercise in Ireland by the Scottish Church of a potent and, as it proved, permanent influence.

1. The first was the "Plantation" of Ulster —an enterprise occasioned by Irish disaffection towards English rule, and by the precipitate flight, after alleged treason, of the Earls of Tyrone and Tyrconnel in 1607. Large tracts of country in that province, extending to about 500,000 acres, were forfeited to the British Crown; and liberal grants of land which, in whole or part, was lying waste through long neglect and frequent warfare, were made over on reasonable conditions to British colonists.[50] The greater share of these territorial concessions fell to the Scots. The spirit of enterprise is characteristic of the Scottish people; Ulster was the home of a large section of their remote ancestors; and the vicinity of Ireland to the south-west of Scotland suggested at once the application for, and the bestowal of, royal grants. That a large proportion of the colonists came from Ayrshire and Wigtownshire is proved by the prevalence of certain names alike in these two counties and in Ulster.[51]

The religious and ecclesiastical outcome of

this migration was most conspicuous. In the beginning of the seventeenth century the population of Ulster was more Roman Catholic than that of Ireland as a whole;[52] and so meagre was the organisation of the Reformed Church, that not only were numerous parishes without Protestant pastors, but three Episcopal sees—Derry, Raphoe, and Clogher—had never been supplied with a Reformed bishop. The share of Scotland in the consolidation of the Protestant Episcopal establishment may be inferred from the fact that, in 1610, five Irish sees were occupied by churchmen of Scottish birth.[53]

The Plantation of Ulster, however, is memorable, in the religious sphere, chiefly as the event which led to the foundation of the Scoto-Irish Presbyterian Church. Up to that time, although individual Presbyterians were found in Ireland, some of them occupying influential positions, Presbyterianism, in any organised form, was non-existent.[54] By a strange irony, the rise of an Irish Presbyterian Church was due to the policy of a king who disliked Presbytery as the supposed foe of monarchy. James I. was then engaged in the process of transforming the government of the Scottish Church into episcopacy; and it suited the scheming king to give, as well as discontented Scotsmen to accept, the opportunity of leaving their native land. The ecclesiastical circumstances, moreover, ensured that the Presbyterian farmers who emigrated from Scotland would be accompanied by an adequate supply of sympathetic spiritual husbandmen. It must be added that, while a portion of the Scottish immigrants were men of moral worth and religious life, the majority appear to have been at first of opposite character; so that, to an earnest Scottish Presbyter, the spiritual condition of his fellow-countrymen in Ireland, even more than his own ecclesiastical discomfort in Scotland, presented a strong motive for emigration.[55] To Ulster, accordingly, there came from the Scottish Church, between 1613 and 1630, most of the men who are venerated as the fathers and founders of Irish Presbyterianism —Edward Brice[56] of Broadisland, who, as minister of Drymen in Stirlingshire, had been a conspicuous opponent of Archbishop Spottiswood; Robert Cunningham[57] of Holywood, described by a younger contemporary as "the man who most resembled the meekness of Jesus Christ that ever I saw"; Robert Blair[58] of Bangor (great-grandfather of the more celebrated Hugh Blair of Edinburgh), an adversary, like Brice, of the prelatists, who had driven him from a Chair in the University of Glasgow; Josias Welsh[59] of Oldstone, afterwards of Templepatrick, son of the more famous John Welsh of Ayr, and grandson of John Knox; James Hamilton[60] of Ballywalter, who at a later stage took the leading part in the propagation of the Solemn League and Covenant; George Dunbar[61] of Larne, who had been twice ejected from his charge at Ayr, and subsequently imprisoned at Blackness for Presbyterian persistency; John Livingstone[62] of Killinchy, great-grandson of the Lord Livingstone who was guardian of Queen Mary, and, like most of the others, a notable opponent of prelacy and of Anglican innovations in his own land.

Fortunately for the Presbyterian immigrants, the head of the Anglican Church in Ireland, during part of this period, was the celebrated Archbishop Ussher, the Leighton of Irish Episcopacy. His laudable attempt, like that of the Scottish prelate half a century later, to effect a union between Episcopalians and Presbyterians, was unsuccessful; and in the closing years of his primacy, between 1636 and 1640, he was unable to prevent the deposition of Presbyterian ministers and the repression of Presbyterian worship under the potent influence of Wentworth and Laud. But, during the critical period of its infancy, Irish Presbyterianism received from Ussher, as Bishop of Meath and afterwards as Archbishop of Armagh, a generous toleration. Under him, indeed, as well as other contemporary prelates, owing mainly to the dearth of Reformed Episcopal clergy, several Presbyterian ministers received the cure of vacant parishes (without renunciation of Presbyterian principles and usages), as a supplementary part of the Anglican ecclesiastical organisation.[63]

2. The second conspicuous impulse to the extension of Scottish Church influence in Ireland, and particularly in Ulster, was given by the massacre of 1641. Whether this massacre was the outcome of a deliberate Romish conspiracy against an aggressive Protestantism,

or, as is more probable, a bloody incident in what was essentially an anti-British insurrection[64] by a conquered and partially dispossessed race, there can be no doubt that in this time of terror thousands of Ulster Protestants[65] were pitilessly butchered, and the foundation was then laid for that religious animosity which prevails in the North of Ireland to the present hour. By this time the relations between Charles I. and the English Parliament had become strained; and that Parliament was not prepared to entrust the king with an army which, after suppressing Irish rebellion, might be used for oppressing English subjects. Charles, moreover, had given some occasion for the dark suspicion, even if in reality unfounded, that he had himself fomented the insurrection in its earlier stage for selfish political purposes. The king, accordingly, solicited the aid of the Scottish Estates, which were then under the control of the Covenanters. The appeal for intervention was favourably received; the necessary sanction of the English Parliament was, after some delay, obtained; and an army of 10,000 Scots was despatched to Ulster, in the spring of 1642, to put down the revolt, and to protect the lives of the Scottish colonists (estimated as nearly 100,000), and of the Protestant population as a whole. Scottish influence in Ulster, thus strengthened, was further promoted by the English regiments already there being placed under the military authority of the Scottish general, Munro.[66]

This expedition in 1642 marks a fresh epoch in the history of Presbyterianism in Ireland. The Irish rebellion had driven out of Ulster most of the Episcopal clergy who escaped the massacre; the Scottish army restored to the North of Ireland Presbyterian ministry and worship. The troops from Scotland, accompanied by Presbyterian chaplains, continued in the country, not only until the insurrection was suppressed, but until all danger of its renewal was over; many, moreover, both of the military and of the ministers, remained as permanent settlers after the conclusion of their temporary work as deliverers. At a time when Scottish influence was thus predominant in Ulster, the opportunity was taken of developing the Presbyterian community into an organised Church. Previously there had been only pastors and congregations holding

Presbyterian views, and more or less tolerated according to the attitude of bishops and governors. During the military occupation, kirk-sessions had been established in the regiments, God-fearing officers acting as elders; and in June 1642 the first formally constituted Presbytery in Ireland came into existence at Carrickfergus. It consisted of five Scottish regimental chaplains, and four officers who also were elders. The organisation thus inaugurated was speedily extended. Seven congregations were organised as a Presbytery of Antrim, eight as a Presbytery of Down. In response to an Irish petition for assistance, the Scottish General Assembly, in the autumn of 1642, sent six deputies to aid in the development of the Presbyterian organisation. The churches became crowded with worshippers; and not a few Episcopal clergy joined the Presbyterian ranks.[67]

3. The third notable impulse to the growth of Scottish ecclesiastical influence in Ireland was given by the Solemn League and Covenant, which was adopted by England and Scotland in 1643. Presbyterianism became, in consequence, the national religion of Great Britain;

and although this ascendency, outside of Scotland, was artificial and short-lived, it lasted long enough to strengthen the influence of the Scottish Church in Ireland. With the joint sanction of the English and Scottish Parliaments, commissioners were despatched to Ulster from Scotland by the General Assembly to administer the Covenant. It is expressly declared by one of the commissioners (Patrick Adair) "that only those whose consciences stirred them up to it" were asked for their signatures; and in many quarters, as might have been expected, opposition was encountered. But enthusiasm for the cause was also widespread; "the Covenant was taken with great affection," and Presbyterian congregations were formed where none had formerly existed.[68] The double impulse, communicated by the expedition of 1642 and the Commission of 1644, was followed, after an interval, by enforced tranquillity under Cromwell. As the outcome of these various influences, the disorganised Presbyterian remnant which had survived the repressive policy of Laud and Wentworth developed into an organised Church of eighty congregations, under the government of a

General Synod.[69] The social disintegration, moreover, and the decay of religion and morals, resulting from the prolonged intestine warfare which the massacre had inaugurated, were effectively arrested by the consolidation and extension, through Scottish agency, of a Church whose discipline, if sometimes severe, was on the whole, in the circumstances, salutary.[70]

III. During the interval between the Restoration of 1660 and the Revolution of 1688, the persecution of Irish Presbyterians, while less severe than that of the Scottish Covenanters, was sufficient to try the constancy of both pastors and people. The illustrious author of the *Liberty of Prophesying*—Jeremy Taylor—led the policy of repression in 1661 by silencing thirty-six preachers within his diocese at his first visitation as Bishop of Down and Connor. Sixty-one Presbyterian ministers in Ulster were ejected, many of them being imprisoned or banished on the ground of nonconformity or on pretence of disloyalty. Presbyterian churches were for a time closed, and the interdicted worship could be conducted only in secrecy. Presbyterian adherents were cited before diocesan courts to answer for non-attendance at Episcopal churches, and were impoverished by heavy fines.[71] Ridicule was added to repression: in a drama entitled the *Nonconformist*, a Presbyterian minister was put into the stocks and held up to unseemly mockery.[72] If, notwithstanding all, the Irish Presbyterians continued steadfast in their testimony, and even propagated their principles in districts of the country previously unreached, such faithful persistency may be ascribed, in no small degree, to the signal example of the Mother Church in her yet fiercer conflict — the example which fugitives from Scotland were constantly reporting in Ireland, of Scottish Covenanters enduring the rude violence of the troopers, the torture of "boot" or thumbscrew, and in many cases death itself, in defence of what they believed to be vital Christian truth.

The influence of the Scottish Church in Ireland was continued in post-Revolution times. An Irish Archbishop, in 1715, estimated that during the previous quarter of a century there had been a fresh immigration into Ulster of fifty thousand Scotch families, attracted by cheap farms or openings for trade.[73] The religious coldness which crept over Scotland, as over Christendom generally, in the eighteenth century, affected also the Presbyterian Church of Ireland. The Arian and Socinian tendencies, which then characterised a portion of the parochial preaching and academic teaching of the Scottish Church, were reproduced in a similar, and eventually more pronounced, deflection from sound faith among the Irish Presbyterian ministers, many of whom received in Scotland their professional training.[74] The Scottish Presbyterian Secessions of the eighteenth century, the controversies which attended them, and the subsequent schisms among the Seceders themselves, reappeared in Ireland, infusing into Irish, as into Scottish, ecclesiastical life at once an earnest and a narrow spirit.[75] The Scottish evangelical movement in the early part of the nineteenth century had as its spiritual counterpart the Irish anti-Unitarian movement, in which Dr. Henry Cooke of Belfast was the successful champion of orthodoxy.[76] The missionary revival in Scotland, of which, as we have seen, Inglis was the pioneer and Duff the apostle, stimulated the establishment, in 1830, of an Irish Presbyterian Missionary Society which, like that of the Mother Church, occupied a field in our Indian Empire.[77] The return of the Scottish Churches, during the present generation, to the use of instrumental music in congregational praise, and (what is of more importance) the increased attention paid in recent years to the devotional services as distinguished from the sermon, has been followed by a similar movement among Irish Presbyterians, with an issue more conservative, indeed, but so far in the same direction. Finally, while a close and cordial intercourse, involving mutual influence, has been maintained, without interruption, between the Presbyterians of Ireland and one or more branches of the Scottish Church, a temporary estrangement of Irish Presbyterianism from the National Church of Scotland, occasioned by the lamentable events of 1843, has recently been happily removed. Ten years ago, a deputation from the daughter

Church received a warm welcome from the Scottish General Assembly, and the bond between Irish and Scottish Presbyterianism became stronger and closer than ever.

It does not concern us here to determine the rightness or the wrongness of the attitude which the Presbyterian Church of Ireland has, with substantial unanimity, adopted regarding the keenly contested question of Irish Home Rule. From the historical standpoint, however, it is pertinent to recognise that (whether for good or for evil), through the influence, in considerable measure, of the Irish Presbyterian Church, the Home Rule policy remains still unaccomplished. Ulster, with its strong Presbyterianism and keen anti-Romanism,[78] with its population of Scottish descent, and its persistent attachment to British connection, has pre-eminently and effectually "barred the way." When the Scottish Church in the seventeenth century spread itself over the North of Ireland with self-propagative activity, it created unconsciously a great force destined to arrest, temporarily or permanently, what some have lauded as a beneficent irenicon, and others have denounced as a pernicious scheme of disintegration, but what all regard as a policy fraught with momentous imperial issues.

LECTURE IV

THE INFLUENCE OF THE SCOTTISH CHURCH AND OF SCOTTISH CHURCHMEN ON THE CONTINENT OF EUROPE.

For six hundred years at least—since the era of the wars with England for national independence—the Scots have been notable among nations at once for loving and for leaving their fatherland. The spirit of enterprise which, in yet earlier times, had signalised the Scottish race as energetic colonists and as missionary pioneers, was fostered and strengthened, in the thirteenth and fourteenth centuries, by prolonged patriotic warfare. Such protracted conflict, by enriching the national character with self-reliance, and impoverishing simultaneously the national resources, led to numerous Scotsmen of varied gifts seeking fame or fortune on continental arenas, military, literary, or ecclesiastical.[1]

When the period of national warfare, moreover, had closed, other conflicts between Catholics and Protestants, between Episcopacy and Presbyterianism, between Church and State succeeded, to swell the stream of enforced or voluntary exile, and to multiply in numberless ecclesiastical spheres the "Scot abroad."

Frequent wars with the English and consequent alliance with the French led naturally to extensive emigration to France. In the century of continuous struggle between France and England, from the battle of Crécy in 1346 to the loss of Cherbourg by the English in 1450, the Scottish auxiliaries of the French army played no inconsiderable or ignoble part. On one occasion, early in the fifteenth century, we read of a host of seven thousand men, under John Stewart, Earl of Buchan, coming from Scotland to the aid of France.[2] In more than one battle with the English invaders the Scots occupied the van; the eventual expulsion of the English is expressly attributed, in a French State document, to Scottish valour; and the standing Guard of Scots at the French Court, as is correctly represented in *Quentin Durward*, enjoyed the confidence of that most supicious of monarchs, Louis XI.[3]

In the less martial, but hardly less contentious sphere of Theology and Philosophy, France presented at this period almost equal opportunities of distinction and service. The ancient University of Paris drew to its lecture-rooms numerous Scottish ecclesiastics, designated one of its four sections of students the "nation" of Germans and Scots,[4] and included in its academic fellowship the Scots College founded by David, Bishop of Moray, in the reign of Robert Bruce.[5] Many of the Scottish Churchmen who came to Paris received much more than they gave, and were the means of transmitting to their countrymen at home potent intellectual and religious impulses. But others contributed even more than they received, and became leaders and moulders of continental religious thought.

I. Even before the era of political alliance between the French and Scottish nations, one illustrious Scot, among others more or less notable,—a Scot, apparently, according to pre-Reformation testimony, in the later sense — occupied in the twelfth century a conspicuous and influential position in France. We refer to Richard of St. Victor[6] (d. 1173), so called from the famous monastery of that name in Paris, and, next to the still more celebrated Hugo, the leading Doctor of the Victorine School of medieval theology. Blending the scholasticism founded by Anselm of Canterbury with the mysticism whose prophet was Bernard of Clairvaux, Richard, along with other theologians of his school, maintained that neither through the mind and argument only, nor through the heart and devout communion alone, but through both agencies in harmonious co-operation, the truths of Divine Revelation are adequately known and realised.

More than a century after the time of Richard of St. Victor, at the epoch of fiercest conflict between Scotland and England, a yet more illustrious Scotsman flourished on the Continent, first in Paris, latterly at Cologne— Duns Scotus (d. 1308). A cloud of mystery overhangs the early life of this great Schoolman, the wonder of his age; and evidence has been adduced in support of the claim of

Ireland, and more particularly of England, to the honour of his nativity. The distinct statements, however, of several pre-Reformation writers, and especially the testimony of John Major, who speaks of the birth of Scotus at Duns, within a few miles of Major's own early home, fix beyond reasonable doubt the connection of Scotus with Scotland.[7] The writings of the "Doctor Subtilis," and those of his great rival Thomas Aquinas, the "Doctor Angelicus" (d. 1274), separated the divines of the fourteenth century into Scotists and Thomists. These two theological giants of medieval Christendom, while maintaining many Romish errors, nevertheless, by setting before the Church the ideal of rational as distinct from blind belief, helped to forge the weapons with which Romanism was afterwards assailed; and the scholasticism of which they were the most brilliant exponents constitutes, notwithstanding grave defects, a leading stage in the development of Christian theology.[8] Through Duns Scotus Scotland has notably influenced Christendom, in the sphere of Mariolatry, down to the present time. The Immaculate Conception of the Virgin was first authoritatively promulgated as an Article of Faith by Pope Pius IX. 1854; it is now, in virtue of the Papal Infallibility decreed by the Vatican Council of 1870, an essential part of the Roman Catholic creed. It was Scotus who, in 1307, against the express authority of St. Bernard and Thomas Aquinas, and in spite of the tacit disapproval of earlier theologians, won for the dogma its inaugural triumph. So completely was he held, at Paris, to have vanquished its assailants, that in 1387 a Dominican friar who disputed against it was declared, both by the University and by the Bishop of Paris, to be a heretic; and in the following century, that University imposed on all her Doctors a solemn pledge to vindicate what was at first rejected as a superstitious error, afterwards embraced by many as a pious opinion, and finally imposed on all as a vital truth.²

Duns Scotus was only the most illustrious of a long succession of Scottish Churchmen who held positions of influence in France during medieval times. In addition to numerous Scotsmen who occupied French benefices, from a princely archbishopric to a

modest curacy; in addition also to a dense
array of regents and doctors connected with
the University of Paris; there are found in
the pre-Reformation records of that seat of
learning the names of no fewer than thirty
Scottish Rectors, during a period when the
Rector at Paris was regarded as the head of
the academic world.[10]

II. Contemporaneous with, and also ante-
cedent to, the extensive migration of Scottish
scholars and clergy to France, was the settlement in considerable numbers of Scottish monks
in Germany. The Celtic mission to Central
Europe in the seventh century was largely
superseded, but was not entirely supplanted,
by the Saxon mission in the eighth. In
several important centres the Irish Scots, who
preceded Boniface and his followers, held their
ground; and in the eleventh and twelfth
centuries, numerous " Scottish " monasteries,
chiefly Benedictine, were founded in various
German towns and cities, including Erfurt,
Ratisbon, Nuremberg, Würzburg, and Vienna.
That these "Scottish" monks came from
North Britain, as well as from Ireland, may
be inferred from the example of monastic

migration which the record of St. Cadroc in the tenth century supplies (Lecture I.), as well as from the fact that, by the close of the eleventh century, the Scots, as a race, were associated mainly with what is now Scotland. St. Cadroe, as we have seen, became a distinguished reformer of monastic life; and, in like manner, the religious fervour and ascetic usages of these somewhat later monkish emigrants gave to their ministry, in particular during the twelfth century, a notable influence, wherever the Teutonic fraternities had fallen away from pristine monastic discipline and zeal. In the opinion of a modern German writer (Wattenbach) who has devoted special attention to the records of those Scottish monks, they anticipated, in some measure, the Home Mission work which was afterwards accomplished by the Mendicant Friars in the early and better period of their history.[11]

III. In the first half of the sixteenth century two celebrated Scottish ecclesiastics occupied conspicuous positions on the Continent — John Major, whom Melanchthon, even when assailing his views, refers to as the acknowledged "Prince of Paris masters," and his still more famous pupil and eventual detractor, George Buchanan.

1. Thirty years of Major's life were spent at Paris in various academic positions. Cultured youths of many lands, who afterwards helped to direct the thoughts and mould the history of their respective countrymen, came more or less under his influence; and even when they diverged widely from his standpoint and teaching, they were quickened mentally, as well as morally, through contact with his keen intellect and vigorous character. Major became the leader in France of the ecclesiastical party, founded in the previous century by Gerson and D'Aillé, which united loyal adherence to the doctrine of the Roman Church with strenuous opposition to papal despotism and urgent demand for practical reform. In France, however, as in Scotland, to which in his old age he finally returned, Major's advanced ecclesiastical views really promoted the Protestantism which he denounced; and he is justly ranked as a real, even if unconscious, "precursor of the Reformation."[12]

Twenty-eight of George Buchanan's best

years, in like manner, were spent upon the Continent, mainly as a Professor in Paris and at Bordeaux, but also for several years in the newly-founded University of Coimbra, in Portugal, where three less notable Scotsmen were his colleagues. At Coimbra his decided Protestantism and influential propagation of anti-Romish ideas brought down upon him the hostility of the Inquisition, and entailed a prolonged imprisonment, which was the means of enriching the literature of Christendom with the most famous of Latin Psalters. Buchanan was more a humanist than a theologian; but his brilliant reputation throughout Europe, as a scholar second only to Erasmus, gave momentum to his Protestant testimony, and rendered him, in academic circles, abroad as well as at home, a potent force on the side of the Reformation.[13]

2. Contemporary with Major and Buchanan were two other Scottish Churchmen, mutually attached friends, whose names are perhaps less familiar, but who exerted considerable influence during the Reformation era, the one in Germany, the other in Denmark.

Alexander Alane was, like George Buchanan,

a pupil of Major at St. Andrews, and became a canon of the Augustinian Priory in that city. When Patrick Hamilton, the proto-martyr of the Scottish Reformation, preached his so-called heresies at St. Andrews in 1528, Alane, who had already distinguished himself by writing a treatise against Luther, undertook to convince and reclaim the heretic. Instead, however, of Alane converting Hamilton, Hamilton converted Alane. Soon after the former's martyrdom, the latter was consigned by his profligate Prior to a noisome dungeon, from which, after protracted ill usage, he at length escaped to Germany. There he was cordially welcomed by Melanchthon, who called him *the* Scot, and metamorphosed his name, according to the fashion of the time, into the Greek Alesius or "Wanderer." First at Cologne, where he aided the elector, Hermann von Wied, in the propagation of the Reformed Faith; then at Wittenberg, where he vindicated against Cochlaeus the reading and free circulation of vernacular Scripture; afterwards at Frankfort-on-the-Oder, where he held for three years a theological professorship, taking part during this period, along with Melanchthon, in the famous Conference at Ratisbon between moderate Protestants and evangelical Catholics; finally at Leipzig, of whose University he was repeatedly Rector, and where he taught assiduously and wrote voluminously for over twenty years; in all these spheres, Alesius was a conspicuous and influential personality in the early history of German Protestantism. He occupied, like his friend Melanchthon, a middle standpoint between Lutheranism and Calvinism; he was also one of the Saxon Protestant divines who were prepared, on certain conditions, to take part in the Council of Trent; and, amid the numerous internal controversies of Reformed Christendom, he was ever, alike at public colloquies and in private communications, the advocate of mutual concession and the apostle of peace.[14]

While Alesius aided the German Reformation, his friend and fellow-countryman, John M'Alpine, became, under the name Machabaeus, a Reforming leader in Denmark. Formerly Prior of the Dominican Monastery at Perth, Machabaeus had embraced Lutheran opinions, and, in 1534, had fled from persecution to

England, whence in 1540 he removed to Germany. At Bremen, where he first resided, he was the instructor in evangelical truth of San Romano, the future protomartyr of the Reformation of Spain. At Wittenberg, which he afterwards visited, he enjoyed the friendship of Luther and Melanchthon, who recommended him to Christian III. of Denmark. When this sovereign, amid clerical opposition, was establishing Protestantism in his kingdom, no one rendered greater service to the cause than the Scottish exile friar. As royal chaplain, he aided the king in the organisation of the Danish Reformed Church. As Professor of Divinity at Copenhagen, he took a leading part in founding a school of Scandinavian Protestant Theology, and in rearing for Denmark a Reformed ministry. As an accomplished linguist, he translated, in concert with three other scholars, the Bible into the Danish tongue.[15]

IV. In the age which followed the Reformation Scotland contributed a considerable number of notable churchmen, both Catholic and Protestant, to continental Christendom.

1. Prior to the Reformation epoch, most of

the Scottish monks culminated, early in the eighteenth century, in the establishment of a professorship at Erfurt, to which a Scottish Benedictine was always appointed until the University itself was extinguished.[17]

2. Early in the seventeenth century, the despotic ecclesiastical policy of James VI. became the occasion of a group of notable Scottish Presbyterians enriching with their service the Reformed Churches of France and Holland. Among these Scottish exiles of standing and influence were Andrew Duncan, who became Professor of Theology in the Huguenot College of Rochelle; John Sharp, who held a similar position at Die in Dauphiné; and John Welsh of Ayr, son-in-law of Knox, who was appointed to a pastoral charge at St. Jean d'Angely in Angoumois, and won from Louis XII. the designation "Mon ministre." John Forbes of Alford (brother of the more famous Bishop Patrick Forbes), and Robert Durie of Anstruther (son of John Durie, Knox's colleague), became pastors in the Dutch towns of Middelburg and Leyden respectively, and received from the Church of Holland the respectful consideration due

to champions in the cause of spiritual independence.[18]

Chief of all whom at this epoch ecclesiastical despotism drove into the service of continental churches was Andrew Melville, the second founder of the Scottish Reformed Church on a distinctly Presbyterian basis, and for more than twenty years the main director of her policy. Prior to his career in Scotland, which began in 1574, he had occupied for several years a professorial chair in Poictiers and in Geneva successively. On his departure from the latter city to serve the cause of truth at home, Theodore Beza, in the name of all his colleagues, had written to the Scottish General Assembly that "the Church of Geneva could not give a stronger proof of affection to her sister Church of Scotland than by suffering herself to be bereaved of him, that his native country might be enriched with his gifts." When King James VI., despairing of the establishment of Episcopacy in Scotland so long as Melville remained there, shut him up for years, on a trifling pretence, in the Tower of London, Huguenot influence and desire for his service eventually procured for him release, and permission to return to the country where his public life had commenced forty-five years before. From 1611, accordingly, until his death in 1622, Melville occupied a theological Chair in the Protestant College of Sedan, over which another Scot, Walter Donaldson of Aberdeen, presided as Principal; and the exiled ecclesiastical leader signalised this latest stage of his illustrious life by vigorous and influential opposition to Arminianism, open and veiled, in the Huguenot Church.[19]

3. Widely divergent from Andrew Melville, in political and ecclesiastical, as well as theological, standpoint, was his younger contemporary John Cameron of Glasgow, who favoured the royal church-policy which Melville opposed, and held a doctrine of passive obedience to rulers which Melville abhorred. Both, however, rendered conspicuous and valued service to the Protestants of France; and Cameron, if less renowned at home than his great contemporary, was still more influential abroad. "The most learned of Scotsmen," according to the testimony of Bishop Hall, Cameron astonished continental scholars—so his admiring pupil

and biographer Cappel informs us—by "speaking Greek as fluently and as elegantly as they spoke Latin." Fully twenty-two years of a comparatively short life (he died at the age of forty-six) were spent on the Continent; four of these years in Chairs of Philosophy at Bergerac and Sedan, ten in a prominent pastorate at Bordeaux, and four as Professor of Divinity in the Huguenot Colleges of Saumur and Montauban. He founded the Saumur School of Theology, whose adherents are often called after him Cameronites, or, after his distinguished pupil Amyraut, Amyraldists. Cameron and his followers held liberal views in Biblical criticism; and they confronted Arminianism not, like Melville and others, with rigid Calvinism, but with a doctrinal compromise, in which the great truth, obscured by ultra-Calvinists, is recognised, that Christ died for all mankind. So important were Cameron's writings considered that, after his death in 1625, all his manuscript works were published at the expense of the National Huguenot Synod. In spite of opposition from more thorough French Calvinists, and charges of heresy by the rival school of

Sedan, Cameronite views obtained sufficiently strong support in France to secure permanent toleration, and they constitute the inauguration of an independent French Protestant theology emancipated from Genevan leading-strings.[20]

V. Somewhat later in the seventeenth century, among other Scotsmen whom ecclesiastical troubles drove, or whom the pursuit of learning or of some religious object drew, to the Continent, two specially signalised themselves by influential service—John Forbes and John Durie.

John Forbes of Corse, the most famous of the "Aberdeen Doctors" who opposed the National Covenant in 1638, was deprived of his professorship three years later for refusing subscription, and in 1644 left Scotland for the Continent, to avoid molestation on account of his opposition to the Solemn League and Covenant. He visited various continental universities, and resided for two years at Amsterdam, where he published in 1645 his great work entitled *Instructiones Historico-Theologicae de Doctrina Christiana*. His theological learning and acumen, in particular his able vindication of Reformed doctrine, as in harmony not only with Scripture but with the best teaching of the early Fathers of the Church, won for Forbes in his lifetime a European reputation among scholars and divines. The re-issue of his works at Amsterdam and Geneva, long after his death, and the use of his "Instructions" in a condensed form, as a text-book in divinity, down to the early part of the present century, attest the notable influence which his writings long exercised in theological circles abroad.[21]

John Durie, son of the Robert Durie whom James VI. drove into exile, was possessed by a grand life-purpose. He was pre-eminently the peacemaker of his age—the age signalised by civil wars in Britain and by the Thirty Years' War on the Continent. For over half a century, from 1628 until his death in 1680, in England and France, in Germany and Holland, in Sweden and Denmark, sometimes at royal courts, and sometimes at Church synods, now through personal correspondence and now through elaborate publications, with an enthusiasm and a persistency which command our reverence, Durie laboured—agonised

—for the great cause of ecclesiastical unity and confederation. He began with an effort to promote union between the Lutherans and Calvinists of Germany; but his aim soon broadened into a comprehensive scheme for a united evangelical Christendom. His method was as bold as his purpose was noble. In an age which produced the Westminster Confession and the later and narrower Swiss "Consensus," Durie proposed, as regards doctrine, that the "philosophical" creeds of the Reformed Churches should be superseded by "a full body of practical divinity," which "might be proposed to all those that seek the truth" as a common Confession of Faith. In an age when his own countrymen (largely as the result of despotic interference) contended about Presbytery and Episcopacy, about forms of prayer and postures at Communion, as pertaining to the essence of religion, he proposed that the names "presbyterial, prelatical, congregational," should be "abolished" as party watch-words, and that, as regards Church government, modes of worship, and "all matters merely circumstantial," the various sections of the "united Reformed Christians should be left free to follow their own light, as it may be offered, or arise unto them, from the general rules of edification." Durie was supported by the sympathy of several potentates, including Gustavus Adolphus and Oliver Cromwell, Frederick V. of Bohemia and Augustus of Brunswick; by a large number of notable divines, including Abbot the English Primate, Archbishop Ussher, and Richard Baxter at home, Grotius, Vossius, and Calixtus abroad; by not a few congresses and conferences in Germany, Switzerland, and the Netherlands. But the active opposition of narrow men in all Churches, and the *vis inertiae* of Protestant Christendom as a whole on such a question, were obstacles fatal to success. Sadly he laments, near the close of his life, that the chief fruit of his long labour was a clearer realisation of the miserable condition of a disunited Church! Yet, even when constrained to recognise that his object was unattainable in his own time, with unfaltering faith and undiminished eagerness he sought compensation for present defeat by preparing the way for future success on a yet wider arena, and by the advocacy of a union embracing all the churches of Christendom. Durie's testimony and toil were not altogether in vain. He was the pioneer of that movement towards Protestant unity which, in the present century, amid some retrograde movements, has made substantial progress. Within living memory there has been accomplished in Germany, so far at least, the union of Reformed and Lutheran Churches for which he had striven two centuries before. Somewhat later, in 1846, his broader aspiration after the unity of the Reformed Church was partially realised, when the Protestantism of Europe, or at least the larger portion of it, stood forth before the world as in some sense one through the formation of the Evangelical Alliance. Within the last twenty years, the stated assemblage in Council, at brief intervals, of delegates from over fifty Presbyterian Churches throughout the world, has supplied a fresh application of the apostolic motto which moulded Durie's life and work: "We being many are one." [22]

VI. Reference has been made, in the present lecture, chiefly to influential representatives of the Scottish Church in continental lands. But that Church in its corporate capacity has, at various stages, played no unimportant part in the history of continental Christendom. The influence of the ancient Celtic Church of Scotland in the evangelisation of central Europe has already been under review (Lecture I.) The indirect bearing of the struggle maintained by the Church of the Covenanters upon continental history will be subsequently noted (Lecture VI.). It remains to consider the influence of the Scottish Church on European Christendom during the Reformation period and in modern times. In the reign of Queen Elizabeth, as was formerly indicated (Lecture III.), the Reformed Church of Scotland had a direct share in the preservation of English Protestantism against political conspiracy and ecclesiastical intrigue. This influence extended, indirectly, to the general cause of Reformed Christendom. The conspiracy against England and the English Reformation, in the latter half of the sixteenth century, was only part of a wider policy through which Popes, Jesuits, and Roman Catholic potentates aimed at the suppression of Protestantism throughout Europe. The varied outcome of that policy included the proposed union of Scotland with Spain through a marriage between Mary Stewart and the son of Philip II., the massacre of over 30,000 Huguenots on St. Bartholomew's Night in 1572, the invasion of England by the Spanish Armada in 1588, the combination of ecclesiastical persecution with political oppression by Spain in the Netherlands, and finally the Thirty Years' War in Germany. In the earlier and more critical stages of that many-sided Catholic conspiracy, one effective barrier, standing in the way of its successful issue, was the thorough Protestantism of the leaders of the Scottish Church, and their unwavering loyalty to the general Protestant cause. Amid the Romanising aspirations of Mary Stewart and the vacillating sympathies of James VI., the Scottish Church and, through its influence, the main part of the Scottish nation could be relied on as permanently on the side of Protestantism in every possible conflict with Catholic power.[23]

VII. In modern times the influence of the Scottish Church, in a portion at least of continental Christendom, has again become conspicuous. Early in the present century (1816-17) the impressive personality and evangelical teaching of Robert Haldane originated at Geneva the religious revival of which (through his direct impulse) Cesar Malan, Merle d'Aubigné, and Frederick Monod were the leaders; and the city of Calvin became once more a centre from which spiritual light radiated throughout French Switzerland and into France. To the same Scottish influence was due, in 1817-18, a religious awakening among the students of Montauban, issuing in the diffusion of evangelical doctrine among their future Protestant congregations. On his return home, Haldane followed up his personal ministry by the foundation, in London and Edinburgh, of the "Continental Aid Society" for the support of itinerant evangelists—the early pioneer of Franco-Swiss Home Mission organisation.[24] The work of Haldane and his Society stimulated British and especially Scottish interest in the Reformed Churches of Europe.

During the half-century now closing, the evangelical Protestants of the Continent, as they themselves readily acknowledge, have received from the Churches of Scotland and from their representatives a cordial sympathy, which has fortified them in their testimony to vital truth amid surrounding Romanism and Rationalism. Their students have repaired in considerable numbers to several of our Scottish Divinity Halls for theological instruction and spiritual incentive; while continental evangelistic enterprises have obtained from the Scottish Churches substantial support, and from the ministers and permanent members of Scottish congregations abroad valued cooperation. The Waldensian Church, in particular, owes to liberal assistance from Scotland, in considerable measure, the increase of its ecclesiastical well-being through the provision of a moderate endowment, and the growth of its spiritual power in Italy through the extension of its missionary organisation.[29] The annual appearance of notable deputies from continental Protestant Churches in the Scottish General Assemblies testifies that those Churches look to Scotland for friendly alliance and sympathy. Nineteen years ago, when the First General Presbyterian Council met in Edinburgh, one representative after another of the continental sister Churches gratefully acknowledged the cheering and sustaining influence exerted upon them, in their struggles and difficulties, by the spectacle of the Scottish Church—a Church which in the past had maintained her position successfully against civil and ecclesiastical despotism, and which in the present continued to maintain her testimony, on the whole with steadfastness, to vital Christian Truth.[26]

LECTURE V

THE INFLUENCE OF THE SCOTTISH CHURCH IN BRITISH COLONIES, PARTICULARLY IN NORTH AMERICA.

THE Sovereign of Great Britain rules over a Greater Britain "on which the sun never sets"; and Scotsmen have ever taken a prominent part in colonial enterprise. The Scottish Church, accordingly, through her individual members and ecclesiastical organisations, has spread forth her branches, propagated her testimony, and diffused her influence in almost every region of the habitable world.

I. As regards Asia, in our Indian Empire, and in numerous towns and districts elsewhere, from Smyrna in the West to Yeddo in the East, the Scottish Churches not only evangelise the native races through about four hundred

European missionaries, but minister, partly through chaplains and other pastors, partly through ordained missionaries, to a British population which includes many thousands of Scotsmen. In India, especially, much-needed witness is thus borne, among European communities, to Protestant and evangelical truth.

In Africa, during the ninety years which have elapsed since Cape Colony came under British rule, and the abolition of slavery throughout the British Empire inaugurated a fresh interest in the negro race, the Scottish Church has made its influence widely felt, not only among the native populations in many regions of the continent, but also among the Dutch and Scottish colonists. To the Dutch Reformed Church in South Africa it contributed a supplementary ministry, a developed constitution, and spiritual independence; for the more recent Scottish settlers it has made a spiritual provision, considerable although inadequate, which appears likely, ere long, to issue in the consolidation of the scattered Presbyterian congregations into a united and fully organised Church.[1]

When Australia, seventy-five years ago,

under the enlightened government of Sir Thomas Brisbane, ceased to be a mere penal settlement, and became the new home of respectable and industrious colonists, the Church of Scotland, under the auspices of the Governor—himself an elder of the Kirk—was early in the field with a Presbyterian pastorate. In 1826, mainly through the energy of John Dunmore Lang, a minister from the Presbytery of Irvine, a miniature Scottish Church was organised, in the form of a Presbytery of New South Wales. From the Church at home came seasonable help, through supply of ministers and contributions of money, as well as unseasonable hindrance, through the propagation of ecclesiastical conflict and schism. Notwithstanding repeated disruption (followed, however, by early reunion), the original Australian Presbytery has gradually expanded into a strong Federal Union of the Presbyterian Churches in the six Australian colonies. This United Presbyterian Church of Australia comprises nearly five hundred congregations, possesses two well-equipped theological colleges, exercises through its clergy and leading laity a conspicuous influence on the social and religious life of the colony, and has taken a prominent part in the evangelisation of the South Sea Islands, notably through the apostolic labours of John Gibson Paton.[2]

The Presbyterian Church of New Zealand is the youngest daughter of the Church of Scotland. Within sixteen years of the foundation of the colony in 1840, Presbyteries of Auckland in the north and of Otago in the south had been constituted—the original organisations out of which have been developed two Presbyterian Churches, independent of each other as to jurisdiction, but associated in a "union of co-operation," and including together over three hundred congregations. The colony of Otago is peculiarly a creation of the Scottish Church. It was founded at Dunedin, in 1848, by 236 Free Church emigrants accompanied by a Free Church pastor; and, after the lapse of half a century, Presbyterianism still "holds the first place" among the religious denominations of the southern province.[3]

In South America, Central America, and the West Indies, through isolated congregations in Buenos Ayres, Brazil, Honduras,

Bermuda, St. Vincent, and elsewhere, the Scottish Church through some one of its branches, provides for Scottish settlers the religious service to which they have been accustomed from childhood; while in British Guiana an organised Presbytery of the Church of Scotland, and in Jamaica, along with Trinidad, a group of Presbyteries, belonging to the U.P. Church, combine with ministry to British colonists pastoral oversight of native and mixed populations—the descendants, in great part, of emancipated slaves.[4]

II. It is in North America, however, especially in what is, or once was, British territory, that the self-propagative influence of the Scottish Church abroad has been most signally exemplified. Among the thirty or more distinct religious denominations which constitute North American Christendom, the Presbyterian Church, or family of Churches, now ranks, numerically, as fourth; the Roman Catholics, Methodists, and Baptists having each a larger membership. The influence of Presbyterianism, however, is much greater than the relative number of its adherents suggests; it holds a place second to none as a factor in the historical development of American Christianity, and is foremost in the theological activity of the New World. Even when the numerical standard alone is applied, the notable fact is disclosed that the total population of the English-speaking Presbyterian communities of North America—estimated at over nine millions—is considerably more than double of that which is attached to the Presbyterian Churches of Great Britain and Ireland.[5] To Scottish influences, direct or indirect, the growth and mould of American Presbyterianism are by universal acknowledgment mainly due. Amid doctrinal and constitutional divergence which has repeatedly developed into schism, the various Presbyterian Churches of the Western Continent have united in recognising the Church of Scotland as the common mother of them all.

The Scottish Church, in the wider acceptation of the term, is also the mother of American Reformed Episcopacy in its fully developed and organised form. The Protestant Episcopate of the United States, whose jurisdiction extends over a population of fully three millions, traces its descent not from the great

Church of England, but from her lowlier Scottish Episcopal sister. Down to the era of the American Revolution, the Anglicans of the New World were strangely left destitute of bishops.[6] At length, in 1783, the clergy of Connecticut spontaneously elected to the office Dr. Samuel Seabury, originally a missionary of the Society for the Propagation of the Gospel, and afterwards a chaplain in the Royalist army during the Revolutionary war. He was sent to England for consecration, but there were "lions in the way." The English hierarchy doubted the propriety of consecrating a bishop for whom the oaths in the English Ordinal were inappropriate, and to whom neither legal diocese nor reliable endowment had been assigned; they were timidly averse, also, to an ecclesiastical procedure which had not received the sanction either of the Connecticut legislature or of the British Parliament. In this dilemma three bishops of the Scottish Episcopal Church—Robert Kilgour, Arthur Petrie, and John Skinner—came to the assistance of the American Church, "venturing," as the last-named, in the spirit of a non-juror, expressed it, " to show more regard to the Acts of the Apostles than to Acts of Parliament." In November 1884, within an "upper room" fitted up as a chapel, in an obscure street of Aberdeen, the memorable consecration took place through which a Reformed Episcopate was communicated to American Christendom.⁷

III. The "Pilgrim Fathers" who came to New England with the *Mayflower* in 1620, and laid the early foundations of British America, belonged to the Congregationalist section of the English Puritans. But, a few years later, two Scottish Presbyters—George Stirke and Patrick Copland—are found ministering to Puritans in the Bermudas;⁸ in 1629, a Presbyterian colony, planted in Massachusetts, was ecclesiastically organised by two English ministers who had been ejected from their charges for nonconformity;⁹ and, during the great formative period of American history, from the middle of the seventeenth to the middle of the eighteenth century, when the British colonies were being gradually developed into the American nation, about one-half of the emigrants were Presbyterians from the first, while others became such through gravitation towards the stronger body.¹⁰ The ecclesiastical stamp impressed upon American Christianity during those hundred years remains, in some degree, to the present hour.

In the growth and consolidation of this predominant Presbyterianism in North America, the Scottish Church, as already indicated, took, directly or indirectly, the principal part. Out of the four thousand Presbyterians, indeed, who are stated to have emigrated to New England between 1620 and 1640,[11] the majority were probably Englishmen, because during that period the motive to self-expatriation was stronger among English than among Scottish Presbyterians. In spite of the ecclesiastical despotism of which James I. was the crafty pioneer and Charles I. the reckless promoter, there were in Scotland, during their reigns, no such drastic dealings with Presbyterian champions as those which in England, under the guidance of Laud and the Star-Chamber, branded, scourged, and mutilated Alexander Leighton.[12] It was otherwise during the latter half of the seventeenth century. After the battle of Dunbar in 1651, Oliver Cromwell despatched Scottish prisoners in shiploads to the plantations of North America, to be sold as bondmen.[13] During the twenty-eight years which intervened between the Restoration of 1660 and the Revolution, multitudes of Scottish Covenanters were either transported to America as a penalty for alleged crime, or sought there a refuge from protracted persecution at home.[14] So conspicuous a source of emigration was Scotland at this epoch, that landowners of New Jersey, anxious to direct the stream into their own channel, anticipated the advertising agencies of later times, and circulated among the Scottish people an attractive description of the territory for sale in their province, with assurances of complete religious liberty.[15]

It was during this period of tribulation in Scotland that Ninian Beale, a God-fearing colonel and an elder of the Kirk, founded a Scottish colony in the district of Maryland where afterwards arose the city of Washington. He attracted to the new settlement two hundred Presbyterian fellow-countrymen, constituted them into a congregation, provided them with a pastor, and afterwards assigned to them land for a church.[16] During the same period, after the battle of Bothwell Bridge, another colony of persecuted Scots under Lord Cardross—many of them persons of high social standing—settled in South Carolina. A large proportion of the professional men in that State were afterwards found to be of Scottish ancestry.[17] In 1685 a hundred refugee Scotsmen, accompanied by two covenanting pastors—Archibald Riddell and John Frazer—who had been allowed to exchange imprisonment for exile, settled in New Jersey on the site which afterwards became Woodbridge;[18] and in a work published by the leader of the party, at the time of their departure from Scotland, incidental mention is made of 290 other emigrants, who had sailed for the same colony from Leith and Montrose in the preceding year.[19] These instances of Scottish colonisation, during the time of persecution, are only samples of many others which have escaped, for the most part, the research of historians.[20]

The number of emigrants from Scotland at this epoch was not more notable than their quality. Among the two hundred and ninety colonists who sailed from Leith and Montrose in 1684 were "gentlemen and merchants of very good repute." The deputy governor of New Jersey, in a letter of the same year, testifies that "the Scots coming now, and settling, advance the province more than it hath advanced these ten years";[21] and what is specially recorded of this colony by Bancroft, the eminent historian, applies more or less to American settlements in general during that period — "Scottish Presbyterians of virtue, education, and courage, blending a love of popular liberty with religious enthusiasm," emigrated "in such numbers as to give to the rising commonwealth a character which a century and a half have not effaced."[22]

IV. The movement which began in Scotland under the impulse of persecution, continued in the more peaceful times which followed the Revolution of 1688. Refugees from tyranny, who had prospered in their western homes, attracted thither fellow-countrymen who desired to join their friends or to escape from poverty. A portion of the members of the ill-fated Darien expedition (1698), including several of the ministers who accompanied the adventurers, found their way, eventually, to New England or other North American provinces;[23] and, in the earlier half of the eighteenth century, extensive Scottish settlements took place both in the northern and in the southern colonies.[24]

Still more conspicuous, during this period, was the influx of Presbyterians, of Scottish descent, from the North of Ireland; for in their case the spirit of enterprise was stimulated by ecclesiastical repression. With flagrant ingratitude for signal service rendered by the men of Ulster at the Revolution, Presbyterians were debarred by the Irish Test Act of 1704 from holding any office in army or navy, excise or post-office, law-court or civic corporation; they were interdicted even from being married by Presbyterian clergy.[25] Large contingents of Scoto-Irish emigrants, in consequence, streamed into New England, Pennsylvania and Delaware, accompanied or followed by Presbyterian pastors from Ulster or from Scotland.[26] The irritation caused by the imposition of ecclesiastical disabilities was supplemented, as an incentive to emigration, by impoverishment due to successive failures of harvest,[27] and by glowing descriptions of material prosperity and spiritual liberty published by colonial agents. A Pennsylvanian historian of the eighteenth century[28] declares that, for a number of years prior to 1750, there emigrated annually to that colony alone about 12,000 Ulstermen, who were nearly all Presbyterians of Scottish descent; and a modern writer estimates that of the Scotsmen who colonised the North of Ireland in the seventeenth century "there are probably three descendants in America for one at home."[29]

V. The predominance of the Scottish element in the early American Presbyterian Church is significantly indicated by the relation and attitude of the latter to the Church of Scotland. A letter from the Synod of New York to the Scottish General Assembly of 1770 declares that "many or most of the first Presbyterian ministers in this country (America) had their education in Scotland." Of eight pastors who composed the earliest constituted American Presbytery—that of Philadelphia—in 1706, at least four, and possibly more, had been trained for the ministry in one of the Scottish Universities.[30] For the American Presbyterians of this period the Church of Scotland is always the "Mother Church" to whom they look for guidance and sympathy, to whose likeness, laws, standards, and usages they ever seek to conform. In 1730 we find the Presbyterians of New York vesting their ecclesiastical property in representatives of the Church of Scotland.[31] A few years later, in 1733, when a number of Pennsylvanian families were about to emigrate to Virginia, a letter addressed to the Governor of that colony by the Synod of Philadelphia describes them as "of the same persuasion with the Church of Scotland."[32] In 1751 the Synod of New York declared itself to be "united with the Church of Scotland in the same faith, order, and discipline," and to enjoy that Church's "approbation, countenance, and favour."[33] Ten years afterwards an American deputation to the Scottish General Assembly described the Presbyterian Church of the colonies as the "young daughter of the Church of Scotland," whose doctrine, discipline, and worship sh had adopted; while one of the deputies, in letter to the Bishop of London, actually designated himself a "member of the Church established in Scotland."[34] In 1763, a minister, with no Scottish connection otherwise, was deposed by the Synod of New York on this among other grounds, that he had "misrepresented the Church of Scotland."[35] In 1770, when the Presbyterians of South Carolina desired to unite with those of New York and Philadelphia, they were informed that the condition of union was the acknowledgment by their ministers of "the standards of the Church of Scotland, which is considered by this Synod as their pattern in general";[36] and in the same year, when it was resolved to correspond with the Protestant Churches of Europe, "it was natural"—so the resolution declared—"first to turn their eyes to the Church of Scotland, to which they are of all others the most entirely conformed, and from which indeed they may be said to have derived their origin."[37]

VI. The Scottish Church, on the other hand, showed from time to time, in a practical way, her maternal interest in American Presbyterianism, and exerted a corresponding influence over its development. During a period when Reformed Christendom was culpably negligent of missionary responsibility, the Church of Scotland began the work of caring for the spiritual interests of the "Scot abroad"—the work which afterwards grew into her Colonial Mission. In 1717, the Synod of Glasgow appointed a collection to be made for the maintenance of ordinances in Pennsylvania; and the amount raised—over £300, a pretty large sum at that time—became the occasion of an annual collection being made for the same object throughout the Synod of Philadelphia.[38] A few years later, in 1724, an appeal was made by the General Assembly on behalf of the Presbyterian Church of New York, and over £400 was realised.[39] Thrice over within eight years — between 1752 and 1760 — we find the Scottish General Assembly enjoining a collection throughout Scotland in aid of the American Presbyterian Church. The amount in each case exceeded £1000, and in the last instance it was supplemented by simultaneous contributions from the congregations of the Burgher Secession.[40] The mission to the Red Indians, founded in 1739 by the Scottish Society for propagating Christian Knowledge, was conducted through American Presbyterian Commissioners; and, under the influence of this stimulus from Scotland, the Synod of New York inaugurated, in 1751, a Foreign Mission of its own.[41] When a native Indian missionary of the daughter Church, Samson Occom, came, in 1766, as a deputy to Scotland, he was received with warm sympathy by the members of the Society for propagating Christian Knowledge, and by other friends of the mission cause. He collected from them fully £2000 for the establishment of an Indian Christian seminary.[42]

VII. The Scottish Church, including the Secession, contributed at this period not only money but ministers. In the majority of cases these went out as volunteers or by private arrangement; but in not a few instances they were sent, in response to appeals, by Church Courts at home which generally defrayed the expenses of outfit and voyage.[43] The Synod and Presbytery of Glasgow were particularly zealous in the supply of ministers, both officially and privately. This was largely due to the sustained interest taken in American Presbyterianism by Principal Stirling of Glasgow University, who was in constant correspondence with the Courts and clergy of the

Church. During his principalship (1701-28) twenty alumni of Glasgow are known to have emigrated to America as Presbyterian ministers; and on many occasions grateful acknowledgment was made of the "great hand he had in projecting and bringing to bear excellent things for encouraging" the "Scottish Church abroad."[44] Out of about 200 American Presbyterian ministers whose labours during the first half of the eighteenth century are recorded, nearly one-third are known to have been connected with Scotland, in most cases as natives of that country, in a few other instances as sons of Scotsmen; the remainder as students at one of the Scottish Universities, or as agents of the Scottish Society for propagating Christian Knowledge. If to these be added those who came from the Scottish colony in Ulster, one-half of the 200 ministers may be said to be the direct gift of the Scottish Church; while of the remaining 100, born in America, a large proportion, doubtless, were of Scottish descent.[45]

Among natives of Scotland were George M'Nish,[46] one of the original members of the first American Presbytery, and the successful leader of the Puritans of New York in their early conflict against episcopalian encroachment; George Gillespie [47] (not unworthy to bear the name of his more illustrious compatriot), whom Whitefield eulogised as a "faithful servant of Christ," and who contended, with equal zeal, in his Presbytery against laxity of discipline, in his writings against infidel doctrine; and, most notable of all, in the third quarter of the century, Dr. John Witherspoon,[48] a descendant of John Knox, who had signalised his early ministry in Scotland by vigorous opposition to Moderatism. In America he became still more celebrated as the President of Princeton College, the perfecter of the Church's constitution, and the one divine who, as a member of the "Continental Congress" of 1770, signed the Declaration of Independence. Among Ulster Scots, trained in Scottish Universities, three names are especially notable. Francis Makemie [49] was the "Father of the American Presbyterian Church" as an organised institution, and the first moderator of its first Presbytery. His imprisonment in 1706 for preaching in New

York without a licence, along with his triumphant acquittal after a memorable trial, constitutes a landmark of American Church History. William Tennent [50] was the founder (in 1727) of the famous Log College, the earliest American seminary for the training of pastors. Along with his three sons, and with the aid of Whitefield, he originated the "Great Awakening" in the second quarter of the eighteenth century; and his earnest endeavour to secure and maintain a godly ministry was the means, notwithstanding some methodistical extravagance, of delivering American Presbyterianism from a stiff and lifeless orthodoxy. Francis Alison,[51] of New London, was "the best Latin scholar of America," the head of a notable training college, and the first theologian of the colonies who received (from the University of Glasgow) the doctorate of divinity. The foremost divine on the conservative side in the first American schism, he was none the less one of the leading promoters of the subsequent ecclesiastical re-union.

VIII. The Church of Scotland had the opportunity, in the eighteenth century, of strengthening the cause of liberal as distinguished from narrow Presbyterianism in America. Up till 1729, the American Presbyterian Church had no formal creed.[52] A large proportion of her pastors, having been licensed or ordained in Scotland or Ireland, had signed, before emigration, the Westminster Confession;[53] and the ministers, as a whole, were united doctrinally, as well as personally, by the bonds of mutual acquaintance, and of confidence in each other's faith. It was inevitable, however, as the number of clergy increased, that this security for orthodoxy should come to be widely regarded as inadequate. Two parties, accordingly, arose in the Church, the one insisting on a formal subscription of the Westminster Creed, the other content to rely on a personal examination of candidates for licence or for ordination. The first outcome of this divergence of view was a pacific compromise. By what was called the "Adopting Act," passed by the American Synod in 1729, the Westminster Confession and Catechisms were adopted "as being, in all the essential articles, good forms of sound words and systems of Christian doctrine"; and every minister was required to signify, either by subscription or by oral assent, "his agreement in opinion with all the essential and necessary articles of the said Confession." The proviso, however, was added, that whoever might have "any scruples with respect to any article or articles" shall be free to declare them on the occasion of his subscription or assent. The power of decision whether the point in dispute were essential, or not, was reserved to the particular Church Court concerned.[54]

This compromise, however, was not universally accepted. Difference of opinion regarding subscription remained, and was associated with simultaneous divergence regarding the Revival movement originated by Tennent and fostered by Whitefield. The issue was the first American Presbyterian schism in 1745. On the one hand were the "Old Side" men, as they were called, who supported strict subscription, and discountenanced the proceedings of the "Great Awakening" as irregular. On the other hand were the "New Side" men, who were liberal subscriptionists, and also cordially recognised the Revival as the work of God.⁵⁵ Which section was to obtain the ascendency? This depended, in no small degree, on the influence of the Churches at home, to which both parties looked for sympathy, and especially on the attitude of the Church of Scotland, the recognised mother of American Presbyterianism.

The Church of Scotland was then in its Moderate era. It had dealt over-leniently, as many considered, with Professor Simson of Glasgow, who had endeavoured, without much success, to harmonise the old doctrine of his Church with the new methods of thought current in his time, and who had been charged first with Arminianism and afterwards with Arianism. Simson had eventually been suspended indefinitely from his office, but had not been deposed from the ministry; while, a few years later, three other suspected divines, Professor Campbell of St. Andrews, Principal Wishart of Edinburh, and Professor Leechman of Glasgow, had all, after trial, been acquitted by the General Assembly.⁵⁶ On the other hand, when Whitefield visited Scotland in 1741 and 1742, many ministers of the National Church cordially welcomed the fervent Methodist to their pulpits, while Seceders, after a vain endeavour to mould him into their ecclesiastical likeness, stigmatised him as an "abjured prelatical hireling," a "servant of Satan," and a "destroyer of the souls of men." [57]

There could be no doubt, accordingly, as to which party among the American Presbyterians would receive more sympathy from the Church of Scotland, and in 1754 that Church had the opportunity, in a practical way, of indicating her attitude. The liberal or "New Side" aimed at the establishment on broad lines of a fully equipped Theological College for rearing a native ministry; and it was to help forward this enterprise that the Church of Scotland, under the guidance of William Robertson, the future Principal of Edinburgh University and historian of Charles V., appointed one of the collections, already referred to, in aid of American Presbyterianism. The Moderate period of the Scottish Church was characterised by many grave shortcomings; but, undoubtedly, on this important occasion, the Church's influence was exerted on the side of genuine liberality, and helped to secure for the broader and more enlightened party in the colonies substantial concessions which eventuated in ecclesiastical re-union.[58] When that Presbyterian re-union was accomplished in 1758 (1) religious "commotions," however "unusual," if "attended with good effects," were acknowledged as the gracious work of God"; and (2) the acceptance and approbation of the Confession of Faith were explained and, so far, qualified by the words "as an orthodox and excellent system of Christian doctrine"; and the duty of resignation, on the part of any who might be found holding views divergent from those of the majority, is expressly limited to such "determinations as the body of the Church, through its Courts, shall judge indispensable in doctrine or Presbyterian government." Since 1825, ministers and elders in the American Presbyterian Church have been ordained after this moderate formula of declaration: "I sincerely receive and adopt the Confession of Faith of this Church as *containing* the system of faith (or doctrine) taught in the Holy Scriptures."[59]

IX. The foundations of the existing Presbyterian Church in what is now British America can hardly be said to have been laid until after the middle of the eighteenth century,[60] when the capture of Quebec, in 1759, terminated French domination in Canada, and opened up fresh fields for British colonising enterprise. From the first a large proportion of the British emigrants were Scots; the Highlands of Scotland, in particular, supplied numerous contingents. Bands of Ulstermen swelled the Scottish stream of colonisation; and, at the close of the American war, the Scottish population was notably increased by the arrival of disbanded soldiers who received grants of lands as rewards for military service, and also by the migration northward of American royalists of Scottish ancestry, who left their old homes in the new Republic rather than lose connection with the mother country and the British Crown.

Some of the communities thus constituted received ministers from the Church of Scotland and from various branches of the Secession; others were supplied with religious ordinances by the Scoto-Irish Presbyterians;

others still were ministered to by Scottish
ex-chaplains of the British army in America,
and by pastors sent from the older colonies
before and after the war. Directly or indirectly, the spiritual provision, no less than
the Presbyterian population for which it was
made, came as a whole from the Scottish
Church;[61] while to Scotland, also, the Anglican communities were indebted for some of
their most influential Church dignitaries.[62]
The formation, in 1825, of the Glasgow
Colonial Society for "promoting the moral and
religious interests of the Scottish settlers in
British America" supplied a definite channel
for the transmission of spiritual influence
from Scotland to our western colonies, and
was the means, within ten years, of forty
ministers being added to the Presbyterian
organisation. In 1836 the establishment by
the Church of Scotland of its Colonial Scheme
placed on a firm basis the support by the
Mother Church of her colonial daughters,
made closer her connection with them, and
increased her influence over them. During
the sixty intervening years, through this
scheme and the corresponding organisation

in the Free Church, the Presbyterians of the Dominion of Canada have received substantial aid, alike in their endeavours, through fully equipped colleges, to rear a cultured Canadian ministry, and in their missionary efforts for the provision of Presbyterian ordinances in new provinces, and in outlying districts of the older colonies.

The influence of the Scottish Church in British North America has, unhappily, not been entirely for good. Secession and disruption at home were reproduced on a smaller scale abroad, without the excuse of protracted conflict and disuniting circumstances. But the growth of friendly co-operation and, to a limited extent, the accomplishment of re-union between certain sections of the Presbyterian Church in Scotland, have also not been without a beneficent and healing influence. In 1875 the Presbyterians of British America, with the exception of some twenty congregations and their ministers, were re-united, it may be hoped permanently, under the name of the Presbyterian Church in Canada, which includes within its pale 755,000 adherents. The number is not widely different from that of the population of Scottish descent in the Dominion, and constitutes 27¼ per cent of the non-Catholic population, as compared with 33¾ per cent who are Methodists, 23¾ per cent Anglicans, and 10¼ per cent Baptists.⁶³ Presbyterianism is thus more than twice as strong in British North America as it is in the United Kingdom, where its adherents number only 12 per cent of the Protestant population.⁶⁴ " Among Protestant denominations" (in Canada) — so a leading Canadian ecclesiastic declares—"the Presbyterian Church stands numerically second, but second in no other sense." In virtue of its social prominence, educational work, philanthropic activity, theological fertility, and missionary enterprise, Canadian Presbyterianism presents a notable and worthy testimony to the influence of the Scottish Church in " Greater Britain." ⁶⁵

X. In the United States, at the present time, Presbyterianism occupies a less important position, numerically, as compared with other Protestant denominations, than in the Dominion of Canada.⁶⁶ A century ago the reverse was the case. At the close of the

Revolution conflict, in which the Presbyterians, as a whole, were zealously on the side of American Independence, Presbyterianism was the dominant religious denomination of the new Republic. Episcopacy, never so strong, owing to the more limited emigration of English Churchmen, had been weakened, during the war, through the attachment of most of its adherents to the Royalist side, through numerous desertions, in consequence, by those who belonged to the Revolution party, and through extensive migration, at the close of the war, to Canada and Nova Scotia. The Baptists and Methodists occupied still a subordinate place; the immigration, on a large scale, of Irish Catholics, through which the Roman Catholic Church has eventually become the strongest religious denomination, numerically, in North America, had not yet begun.[67] That the Methodist and Baptist Churches have each outstripped the Presbyterian during the present century, as regards numbers, is due partly, perhaps, to Calvinism deterring Englishmen who on other grounds would have been attracted, but has resulted chiefly from the strictness of Presbyterian regulations regarding ministerial training. The Presbyterian Church found itself unable adequately to provide a fully educated ministry for the fresh communities which were constantly springing into existence, and it declined to license and ordain those whom it regarded as imperfectly qualified candidates for evangelistic and pastoral ministry.[68] Presbyterianism was thus gradually superseded by the more elastic and adaptable organisations of Methodists and Baptists, in the provision of religious ordinances not only for English but for Scottish colonists. To the emotional populations of African descent, on the other hand, the graver character of Presbyterian worship was less attractive than the livelier and more varied religious service which rival denominations supplied.

There remain, however, to the present day, in American Christendom as a whole, notable fruits of the preponderant influence exerted by the Scottish Church — its testimony and traditions, its usages and characteristics — in the century during which Presbyterianism contributed a full half of the emigrant population, and much more than one-half of its intellectual power and religious earnestness. To such early Presbyterian impressions it is mainly due that in the United States (outside the Roman Catholic Church) episcopacy occupies, as yet, a comparatively subordinate place. To the same cause may be traced the two notable facts that sacerdotalism, whose recent progress in Great Britain is so remarkable, has taken no signal hold of the American Reformed Church, and that in all the leading Protestant denominations (the Episcopalian included) there is a more or less ample recognition of the lay element in Church government.[69] To Scottish influence, mainly (along of course with that of the English Puritans), may be traced the further fact that, throughout a large portion both of British America and of the United States, what are termed Scottish ideas of Lord's Day observance continue to maintain their ground.[70] In the States, no less than in Canada, a large share of the missionary and philanthropic enterprise of the nation, and a yet greater proportion of its theological and apologetical literature, belong to the Church which still recognises the Church of Scotland as its ecclesiastical mother.⁷¹ To Scottish example, and to Presbyterian enterprise and religious earnestness, are largely due two features of the American educational system which otherwise might have been less prominent: on the one hand, the wide extension of the benefit of University education among a people whose history and circumstances might not unnaturally have led to the sacrifice of intellectual culture to material prosperity;⁷² on the other hand, the conservation of Christian teaching—speaking generally—as an integral part of the public school curriculum, in a country where the principle of religious equality is not only asserted but emphasised.⁷³ To Scottish traditions, finally, which, up to a date within living memory, were almost wholly antagonistic to the voluntary principle in religion, is largely to be ascribed the survival of not a little which bears witness to National Religion in a country where Voluntaryism, through force of circumstances, has been universally adopted in practice, and generally, also, in theory. Such witness is borne by the legal recognition of the Lord's Day, by the treatment of blasphemy as not merely a sin but a crime, by the religious services connected with Congress, and by the oath exacted from all servants of the State, from the President of the Republic downwards, at the time of their entrance upon office.

Such notable features of American Christianity and religious life may all more or less be traced, directly or indirectly, to that period of predominant Presbyterianism when the Scottish Church, with its keen anti-prelacy and anti-sacerdotalism, its strict Sabbath observance, its popular University system, its maintenance of a high standard (relatively) of clerical training, and its stanch adherence to the principles of national religion and national religious education, was the paramount influence in the development and moulding of American Christendom.

LECTURE VI

INFLUENCE OF THE SCOTTISH CHURCH IN THE
PROMOTION OF POLITICAL LIBERTY AND
SPIRITUAL INDEPENDENCE.

St. Columba, the founder of the Scottish
Church, was also one of the earliest champions
of Scottish independence. Prior to his settlement in Iona, the ruler of the Scoto-Irish
colony (in Argyll), which afterwards expanded into the kingdom of Scotland, was a
tributary of the King of Dalriada in the
North of Ireland, from which the colonists in
preceding generations had gone forth. On
the death of King Conall in 573, St. Columba,
in accordance—so his early biographer declares—with a thrice-repeated divine intima-
tion, selected Aidan, the cousin of Conall, as
successor; and, without waiting for Irish
sanction, solemnly installed the new king at

Iona.[1] To this bold proceeding, and to the saint's influential support of Aidan's claim to independent sovereignty in the great Irish Convention of 575 at Drumceatt in Derry, was mainly due the recognition thenceforth of the Scottish colony in North Britain as an independent realm.[2] The circumstance is memorable not only on its own account, but for its emblematic significance. Throughout the history of Scotland the Scottish Church has been generally on the side of national independence as well as constitutional liberty, and has borne against despotism, both external and internal, a notable testimony which has potently influenced the history of Britain, and, more or less directly, that of other lands.

I. At two critical epochs, the Scottish Church intervened with signal effect and far-reaching influence in the cause of freedom : first, in the era of struggle with England for national independence, under Wallace and Bruce; afterwards, in the age of conflict with the Stewart kings for civil and religious liberty.

The Scottish Wars with the English people and their kings, in the thirteenth and fourteenth centuries, were preceded by an ecclesiastical conflict, in the twelfth century, with the English Church and her prelates. During this early period of the Roman Church of Scotland, free admission of Anglican influence was remarkably united with resolute resistance to Anglican aggression. The Scottish Church welcomed English clergy to its benefices, English monks to its abbeys, English forms into its worship, English architecture into its church-building enterprise; but of Anglican domination it would have none. English ecclesiastical aggression manifested itself in a claim by the Archbishops of York and of Canterbury to jurisdiction over the Scottish Church, corresponding with the later claim by Edward I. to suzerainty over the Scottish kingdom;[3] and the patriotic Scottish churchmanship which withstood the English primates was a moral preparation for the patriotic Scottish nationalism which, more than a century afterwards, resisted the English King. The Council of Northampton in 1176, at which, under the presidency of a papal legate, the Church question was fully discussed, and the ecclesiastical independence of

Scotland virtually secured,[4] not only foreshadowed, but helped indirectly to bring about, the Treaty of Northampton in 1328, when, in the reigns of Robert Bruce and Edward III., Scotland's political autonomy, after thirty years of struggle, was reluctantly but distinctly recognised. Scottish ecclesiastical independence was formally ratified, in 1188, by a Papal Bull which declares that the "Church of Scotland is a daughter of Rome by special grace, and subject to Rome without any intermediary."[5]

II. The influence of the Church of Scotland, however, on the side of national independence was more direct and conspicuous when the conflict with England actually began. Blind Harry, indeed, in his *Wallace*, composed nearly two centuries after the events described, represents that

> The byschoprykis inclynyt till his (Edward's) croune,
> Bathe temporalite and all the religionne (B. x. 1001-2)

—both the clergy who belonged and those who did not belong to the religious orders. But the poet chronicler, writing amid a popular environment which ecclesiastical abuses had by that time rendered hostile to the Scottish hierarchy, is no more to be trusted here than where he declares, against clear historical evidence, that Edward I. forced on the Scottish Church the Anglican "use of Sarum."[6] No doubt the oath of allegiance to Edward was frequently taken by Scottish bishops; but in every instance, so far as appears, this was done under constraint or menace. It meant no more than that the Scottish prelates had not the devotion of martyrs as well as the zeal of patriots.[7] Nevertheless, the sympathies, influence, and, on many occasions, active efforts of the leading clergy throughout the period of conflict were on the patriotic side; and amid the frequent vacillation and occasional treachery of Scottish nobles, not a few of whom, in virtue of estates south of the Tweed, were also English subjects, the uniform support given by the Scottish prelates to the patriotic cause contributed largely to its ultimate success.[8]

At the Norham Convention in 1291, with which English aggression began, when Edward I. advanced his claim to lordship over Scotland, and when the Scottish nobility were subserviently silent, a Scottish bishop, Wishart of Glasgow, boldly declared in the aggressor's presence, that "the kingdom of Scotland had from the first always been free, and owed homage to none but God and his vicegerent on earth."⁹ Five years later, in 1296, when the servile King Baliol was driven at length, by Edward's overbearing attitude and intolerable demands, to renounce his allegiance, a leading ecclesiastic, Henry, Abbot of Arbroath—"a bold-spirited man," as Bower the annalist calls him—dared the lion in his den, and at the risk of his life delivered to Edward at Berwick the instrument of renunciation.¹⁰ In the following year, when William Wallace inaugurated his patriotic enterprise, one of his leading supporters was the Bishop of Glasgow already mentioned, who, regardless of the charge of sacrilege, devoted the oak-wood which he had obtained for the spire of his cathedral to what he considered the more urgent purpose of constructing military battering-rams.¹¹ Lamberton, Bishop of St. Andrews, the head of the hierarchy, although under constraint he repeatedly swore fealty to Edward, zealously supported the national movement under both Wallace and Bruce. He was ambassador of the former at the French Court, and was the very first man of high position who encouraged Bruce in his patriotic aspirations.[12] It was through the influence of the Scottish clergy that Pope Boniface VIII. was induced in 1300 to intervene on the side of Scotland, and to enjoin upon Edward the cessation of hostilities; although two years later—through English bribes, it was maintained—the same Pope, with discreditable tergiversation, denounced the patriotic bishops as "abettors of disturbance and discord detrimental to their country and displeasing to God."[13] In 1309, five years before the battle of Bannockburn, when Robert Bruce was still simultaneously struggling against English domination and hampered by the jealousy of Scottish nobles, a General Council of the Scottish Church met at Dundee and issued "to all the faithful in Christ" a bold and timely manifesto, in which they render "due fealty" to Bruce as "King of Scotland"; and declare that "with him the faithful of the kingdom will live and die."[14]

The dignitaries of the Scottish Church shared fully—over fully, it must be admitted—in the martial spirit which characterised the patriotism of the time. Wishart of Glasgow held Cupar-Fife against English besiegers, who captured him there in 1306, along with Lamberton of St. Andrews, and the Abbot of Scone, all three being in full armour.[15] David, Bishop of Moray, who afterwards founded the Scots College at Paris, preached publicly that it was no less meritorious to rise in arms against the English for the freedom of Scotland, than to engage in a crusade against the Saracens for the recovery of Palestine.[16] Of another prelate — St. Clair of Dunkeld—it is related that in 1317, when an English force had landed at Inverkeithing, and had driven a band of Scots in full flight before them, St. Clair came to the rescue on horseback, exclaimed to the fugitive leaders, "Our Lord the King would do well to hack your gilt spurs from off your heels," rallied the Scots with the cry "All who love King and country, follow me," and drove back the English invaders to their ships with the loss of 500 men.[17] Every Scottish schoolboy is familiar with the description of the patriotic Abbot of Inchaffray, on the morning of the battle of Bannockburn, passing from rank to rank of the Scottish host, with crucifix in his hands, exhorting the kneeling soldiers to fight bravely for freedom and fatherland;[18] and it is not without significance that the Scottish poet who, in the fourteenth century, chiefly expressed and conspicuously stimulated the patriotic sentiment of the people, was no secular minstrel, but John Barbour, Archdeacon of Aberdeen.

The patriotic spirit and influence of the Scottish Church, at this critical epoch of national history, is strikingly illustrated by the refusal of the clergy to endorse the repeated papal ban against Bruce, first in 1306, after his slaughter of Comyn in the Greyfriars' Church at Dumfries, and later, in 1320, when Bruce refused to open sealed letters from the Pope which were not addressed to him as King of Scotland. That the papal excommunication, even after the double crime of murder and sacrilege, remained innocuous, and that the simultaneous papal interdict, debarring Scotland from priestly ministrations, proved futile, was due to the recognition, notwithstanding all, of Robert Bruce by the Scottish clergy, as a divinely-raised-up champion of national independence, to whom they were ready loyally to adhere not only against the carnal power of England, but against the spiritual fulminations of Rome.[19] This patriotic attitude is finely depicted by Sir Walter Scott in his memorable description of the interview between Bruce and the Abbot of Iona, when the "sainted man from sainted isle" is represented as purposing at first to curse, but constrained, like Balaam, by an inward impulse to "turn the curse into a blessing"—

> "De Bruce! I rose with purpose dread
> To speak my curse upon thy head; . . .
> But, like the Midianite of old,
> Who stood on Zophim, heaven-controlled,
> I feel within my aged breast
> A power that will not be repressed.
> It prompts my voice, it swells my veins,
> It burns, it maddens, it constrains!—
> De Bruce, thy sacrilegious blow
> Hath at God's altar slain thy foe:
> O'ermastered yet by high behest,
> I bless thee, and thou shalt be blest."
>
> *Lord of the Isles*, ii. 31.

There can be no doubt that in that age of conflict, when the secular leaders of the Scottish people were often politically double-minded and suicidally jealous of each other, the uniform support of the national cause by the Church's official representatives had no small share in the deliverance of Scotland from the demoralising humiliation of foreign conquest.

III. The beneficent issues, notwithstanding temporary hardships, of the Scottish Wars of Independence were not confined to Scotland. The long conflict promoted indirectly the cause of constitutional government, and even of national independence, in England. Contemporaneous with the external struggle of Scots against English, was an internal contest of the people of England with their own sovereign for political rights and liberties. In proportion as the Scottish War demanded fresh supplies of men and money, the tenacity of the English King, in regard to what he regarded as royal prerogative, relaxed. The victory of Wallace at Stirling Bridge in 1297 was followed immediately in England by important royal concessions as to taxation; and the prolonged resistance of Scotland to English aggression forced Edward I. to complete the programme of the Magna Charta. In order to obtain fresh equipments, he consented to invest the Commons with that parliamentary privilege of granting or withholding supplies which became a vital part of the British constitution, and a main safeguard at once against useless wars and against baneful despotism.[20]

IV. Not only the constitutional government, but even the continued national independence, of England was intimately connected with that Scottish resistance which the leading Churchmen of Scotland largely helped to render ultimately successful. Had the influence of the Scottish clergy been thrown into the scale of submission to England, and had Edward I. been thereby enabled to reduce Scotland to permanent subserviency, one can scarcely doubt that the subsequent warfare between England and France would have had a very different issue. As it was, France narrowly escaped complete subjugation by the English Kings Edward III. and Henry V., in the fourteenth and fifteenth centuries. But for the Franco-Scottish alliance, the constant danger to England on the Scottish frontier, and the frequent need of part of her strength being occupied in warfare with Scotland, it is highly probable that the Norman-English kings would have become permanently, what they were temporarily, the rulers of France.[21] Are we then to ascribe French national independence partly to the patriotic conflict in Scotland? Primarily, yes; but English independence might eventually have been imperilled, and was, in reality, at this epoch secured. For, what would have been the ultimate issue of England and France becoming permanently under one king and one administration? It is not difficult to discern. Not insular and (as it then was) remote London, but continental and central Paris would have become the seat of government, the habitation of the Court, the fountain of honour, the reservoir of wealth, the focus of influence. Not English, as yet only a half-formed tongue, but French, which was still the language of the English Court, would have been the dominant speech of the united kingdoms; and the writings of Shakespeare and Addison would have been composed in a mere provincial dialect. The wholesome fusion of Saxon and Norman, then being gradually effected, would have been detrimentally interrupted, and would have been replaced by the amalgamation—fatal for England—of Norman with French. The new empire thus created would have been Franco-Norman in name, policy, and spirit; and England would ere long have subsided into the chief appanage of a magnified France.[22] No weightier words were ever uttered by the late Dr. Arnold of Rugby than those in which he declared that "two of the greatest defeats we (English) ever suffered have been two of our greatest blessings—Orleans and Bannockburn;"[23] and to the issue at Bannockburn, of which the series of salutary reverses, inaugurated at Orleans in 1429, were in part the indirect result, the patriotism of Scottish Churchmen influentially contributed.

V. Three centuries have passed since the Wars of Independence. Both in Scotland and in England the Church of Rome has given place to the Church Reformed. The union of the two crowns, which Edward I. and Henry VIII. had vainly attempted to achieve, the former by force, the latter by craft, has been peacefully and honourably consummated under a Scottish king with English ancestry. Once more, in the foreground of the political, as well as the ecclesiastical arena, stands the Scottish Church, as the determined and eventually successful antagonist of royal despotism.

For this later conflict in the cause of liberty two notable Scottish Churchmen, already referred to in another connection, had effectively paved the way, although both were dead before the struggle began. They were both pupils of the illustrious John Major. Major was not merely a Churchman but a politician; and his political views were more advanced than his ecclesiastical. In his *History of Greater Britain* he declares that " from the people kings have their institution," and " on them royal power depends." " The nation as a whole," he writes elsewhere, " is above the king, who exists for the people's good, not they for his."[24] One of the two eminent pupils of Major, who developed and popularised his political creed in Scotland, was John Knox. In the audience of his sovereign, Knox boldly maintained the lawfulness of resisting, deposing, and punishing rulers who transgressed the laws or oppressed the people.[25] These principles received practical application during his life in the deposition and imprisonment of Mary Stewart; and eighty years after his death, John Milton appealed to his writings when vindicating the execution of Charles I.[26] The other of the two pupils was George Buchanan, whose reputation as a humanist and as a historian is not more memorable than his influence as a political economist. In his work *De jure regni apud Scotos* (published in 1579) the principles of constitutional, as distinguished from absolute monarchy, are expounded and defended with a freedom which caused the Scottish Parliament in 1584 to declare the possession of the volume penal, and moved the University of Oxford, a century later, to commit the treatise publicly to the flames.[27] The large circulation which the publication received, and the numerous answers which it drew forth in Scotland and England, and even on the Continent, attest its importance as an epoch-making work, which helped to mould the political opinions of influential thinkers both at home and abroad.[28]

VI. The struggle of the Scottish Church against the despotism of the Stewarts extended over four reigns and lasted for nearly a century, terminating with the Revolution of 1688. To the more distinctively ecclesiastical phase of the conflict reference will afterwards be made. Equally important, and farther-reaching, probably, in its influence, was the political issue of the contest, as a struggle, not less real because at the time not fully realised, for constitutional liberty. Beneath the resistance of the Scottish people in the seventeenth century to "black" prelacy and Laud's Liturgy, to kneeling at Communion and the observance of Christmas, there lay the national determination not to let either religious usage or anything else be forced upon Scotland by arbitrary power, especially when imposed in English form. The struggle was a renewal of the conflict for Scottish Independence, and along therewith a contest for constitutional government. The objection of the Scots to the ecclesiastical policy of the Stewarts, in the earlier stages, at least, of the conflict, was sharpened by the consideration that the government and worship of the Scottish Church were being Anglicised, in order to secure religious conformity in the two kingdoms, as a means towards political consolidation. To a patriotic people, among whom the memories of former wars with England survived, such an Anglicising policy was in itself offensive. It had too much the appearance of a token of Scottish vassalage, such as the proud patriotism of men descended from the victors of Bannockburn and the heroes of Flodden could ill endure.[29]

Deeper, however, than any antipathy to particular forms of worship or modes of Church government—deeper, also, than any resentment against Anglican intrusions, was the spirit of resistance to despotism. When Andrew Melville and other ecclesiastical leaders, in the end of the sixteenth and in the beginning of the seventeenth century, opposed the insidious policy through which James VI. eventually established prelacy; when Calderwood and other churchmen, in 1617, protested against the same King's attempt to abolish the legislative functions of the General Assembly; when, a little later, one-half of the clergy and the majority of the people, led by Scot of Cupar and Dickson of Edinburgh, resisted the

Five Articles of Perth, whose civil and ecclesiastical enactment was obtained by royal intimidation; when, finally, under Charles I., the ministers under the leadership of Henderson, the influential laity guided by Lord Rothes, and the populace stirred by the riot of 1637 in St. Giles's, withstood the imposition of Laud's Service-Book, and organised the movement which culminated in the Covenant — there underlay all objections to those innovations in themselves an equal or graver objection to their despotic introduction by the will of the monarch, and to their high-handed enforcement by the odious High Commission.[30]

VII. In this political bearing of the long ecclesiastical conflict in the seventeenth century, the Scottish Church exerted an influence in England, as well as in Scotland, and, indirectly, in other lands. To the example and influence of the Church of Scotland were largely due the inauguration, prosecution, and successful conclusion of the long political struggle between the English people and the Stewart dynasty —the struggle whose early outcome, when national sympathies were divided, was the Great Rebellion, and whose eventual issue, when the nation had become virtually unanimous, was the British Revolution. When the Scottish Covenanters continued to sit in the Glasgow Assembly of 1638, after the Royal Commissioner had dissolved it in the King's name; when they proceeded, with reforming zeal, to demolish those ecclesiastical innovations and (as they believed) deformations, which the despotism of thirty years had introduced into the Church's edifice; when they took forcible possession of Edinburgh and Dumbarton Castles, and raised a large army to vindicate the Church's testimony; an example of resistance to tyranny was set which fanned the flame of English opposition to unconstitutional taxes, and of indignation against the abuse of royal prerogative, until resentment and remonstrance developed into revolt. Thirty thousand armed Covenanters sitting down on Duns Hill, became, as Carlyle epigrammatically expresses it, "the signal for all England rising up."[31] Within two years of the Duns demonstration, Charles had been constrained to send Strafford to the scaffold; one year later the Civil War began.

As the conflict in England was partly inaugurated, so it was largely sustained through Scottish influence. On the struggle against royal despotism, the Church of Scotland bestowed an ecclesiastical benediction, instead of pronouncing, like the Church of England, through leading representatives, a spiritual ban. The clergy of the former Church, unlike those of the latter, distinguished clearly, in their policy, between conservative resistance to royal tyranny and that radical antagonism to monarchical government whose earlier outcome was a short-lived Republic, and whose later issue was a reactionary Restoration. The Scottish Church helped thus to forward what her English sister for two generations hindered, the growth of constitutional monarchy.[32] Amid prevalent English subservience during the reign of Charles II., Scotland, under cruel persecution, held aloft the banner of the Covenant; and that banner notwithstanding the intolerance of Covenanters, led to liberty, and, amid regrettable extravagances, enlisted in the cause a line of devoted martyrs like Renwick, and a group of patriotic politicians like Carstares. During the struggles, moreover, which attended and, at more than one juncture,

endangered the Revolution settlement, the
Scottish Church contributed potently to the
success of the enterprise by keeping Scotland,
as a whole, on the side of William of Orange
and National Liberty; while in Ireland, but
for the courageous support of the Revolution
by Scoto-Irish Presbyterians, in contrast with
the widespread vacillation (at first) of Anglo-
Irish Episcopalians, James would have retained
his Irish, and might have eventually regained
his English and Scottish kingdoms.[33] Throughout the half-century which elapsed between the
signing of the Covenant and the Revolution,
while dignitaries of the Church of England
sided with despotism, persistently upholding
the divine right of kings and the duty of submission even to a Nero, the Scottish Church,
in spite of its intolerance and occasional fanati-
cism, united loyalty to the monarch's person
with resistance to monarchical oppression, testified against both republicanism and absolutism,
and promoted, if not always intentionally, on
the whole effectually, the cause of civil and
religious liberty. If it be too much to assert
that, but for the Scottish Church, there would
have been no British Revolution, it is safe to

affirm that to the persistent struggle of the earlier Covenanters and the faithful martyrdom of the later, the growth of the spirit which led to that great crisis was largely due.

VIII. The Revolution of 1688 is the acknowledged turning-point of modern political history. It was the signal repudiation by the British nation, before the world, of the "divine right of kings to rule wrong." It was the first stage in the realisation of George Buchanan's maxim that the fountain of political authority is the popular will, and that the end of political government is the popular welfare. In contributing to the success of the Revolution, accordingly, the Scottish Church promoted indirectly the downfall of despotism and the growth of virtual democracy throughout the civilised world. When Great Britain herself, against the counsel of her wisest statesmen, attempted, in the eighteenth century, to impose oppressive laws on her American colonies, the event of 1688, and the education of the preceding half-century, made submission impossible for descendants and kinsfolk of men who had struggled successfully against tyranny at home. The American Revolution was the natural and necessary outcome of the British. Scottish exiles and immigrants, in particular, had carried with them across the Atlantic those instincts of liberty and (in the broad sense) liberalism which the suffering Church of Scotland had fostered. It is amply attested by contemporary royalists, as well as by republicans, in the American conflict, that the earliest and most strenuous opponents of British despotism and promoters of colonial freedom were the descendants of the Scottish or Scoto-Irish Presbyterians.[34] The bronze statue of Dr. Witherspoon, erected at the centennial celebration of American Independence, commemorates the significant fact that the minister of religion who took the foremost part in the struggle was a Scottish Presbyterian divine.

The connection of the British with the French Revolution was less direct and less vital, but can be distinctly traced. In so far as that terrible event was the outcome, not of the lawless passion of the hour, but of a prolonged grievance and struggle against despotism, the chief external impulse was communicated by the signal achievements and testimony of 1688. When the national splendour, which

veiled the oppressive absolutism of the French
monarchy and the luxurious selfishness of the
French aristocracy, passed away, like a transient
vision, with Louis XIV., in 1715, and when
France awoke from her dreams of glory to find
herself a veritable land of bondage, it was to
the British Revolution and Constitution that
leading Frenchmen turned their gaze at once
for an example and for inspiration. British
political ideas permeated France through trans-
lations of English writings ; leaders of French
thought and society acquired, through travel
and social intercourse in England and Scotland, a taste for political liberty; and when
a sufficient inflammatory mass had been ac-
cumulated, the conflagration was hastened by
the successful American Revolt, to which men
of Scottish descent had powerfully contributed.[35] If the Revolution of 1789, like a
destructive hurricane, made shipwreck of much
that was precious, both socially and religiously,
it none the less cleared the political atmosphere
of a great deal that was noxious and noisome.
It paved the way, throughout Europe as a
whole, for a new and better political dispensa-
tion, in which the responsibilities of the ruler,

for the ruled and to the ruled, are more clearly realised, and a beginning has been made with the fulfilment of our Lord's pregnant words: "He that will be great among you, let him be your servant."

IX. Hardly less notable than the influence of the Scottish Church in the promotion of political liberty has been its sustained testimony regarding spiritual independence; *i.e.*, the freedom of the Church, through her courts and councils, from external control within the spiritual sphere.

The witness of the Scottish Church to this principle dates from the earliest period of her organised existence, relates to her attitude towards papacy as well as magistracy, and has been maintained—with virtual unanimity down to the early part of the present century—along with adherence to the principle of Church Establishment. The Church of St. Columba, in the sixth century, was altogether independent of Rome. In the seventh century, that Church, rather than appear to recognise Roman authority and jurisdiction respecting the date of Easter, withdrew from her Anglo-Saxon mission field.[36] This spiritual independence, as regarded the Roman See, continued down to the time of Queen Margaret, when Anglican influences led to the Church's submission to Roman supremacy. Even after the Church of Scotland became Romanised, it was for long conspicuous for its resistance to papal encroachment and uninvited intervention. In the thirteenth century papal legates were excluded from Scotland, and the Pope's demand for crusading tithes was refused.[37] In the fourteenth century, as we have already seen, the Church and her clergy ignored repeatedly the pontifical ban, when Rome interfered with the Scottish national cause.

In post-Reformation times, the Scottish Church, emancipated from papal jurisdiction, maintained, amid recurrent conflict, its spiritual independence against royal encroachment. Under the leadership of Andrew Melville it resisted, with eventual success, the attempts of Morton and of Lennox to reimpose a hierarchy upon Scotland without the authority of the General Assembly. James VI. succeeded in restoring Episcopacy and introducing certain Anglican usages, only through the employment of "kingcraft" to obtain the semblance of the

Church's sanction; while Charles I., by endeavouring to impose ecclesiastical innovations without ecclesiastical ratification, provoked a conflict out of which the Church emerged triumphant. "There are two Kings," were Andrew Melville's oft-quoted words to James VI., "and two kingdoms in Scotland. There is King James, the head of this commonwealth, and there is Christ Jesus, the King of the Church, whose subject James VI. is, and of whose kingdom he is not a king, nor a lord, nor a head, but a member."[38] Throughout the prolonged struggle of the Church with the Stewart dynasty, her fundamental protest, amid varying details, was ever this, that the spiritual jurisdiction of the Church, through her General Assembly, was being unconstitutionally interfered with by the civil power; and the Assemblies of 1638 and 1690, apart from their particular enactments, derive their main importance as landmarks of Scottish Church History from this, that they signalise the recovery of her lost spiritual independence.[39]

During the eighteenth century, while in the re-established Presbyterian Church the question of spiritual independence retreated for a time into the background, the nonconforming episcopal remnant, partly through its severance from the State, partly through the non-juring attitude of its clergy, threw off the Erastianism by which Scottish Episcopacy had formerly been characterised, and adopted ideas of spiritual independence which survived its Jacobite proclivities.[40] In the case of the Presbyterian Seceders, the principle of ecclesiastical autonomy, which they carried with them out of the Church, was increasingly emphasised amid continued disconnection from the State, until, almost within living memory, it developed into Voluntaryism.

In subsequent times, when those internal conflicts began which issued in the lamentable Secession of 1843, the cause of contention, it must be remembered, was not whether the Church possessed spiritual independence and a free ecclesiastical jurisdiction, but whether, in particular instances, she had, or had not, stepped out of her spiritual province, and arrogated to herself civil powers. While the Free Church, accordingly, by making spiritual independence her watchword, bore specially prominent testimony against erastian interference with the Church in her spiritual province, the General Assembly of the Church of Scotland, on the other hand, in a pastoral address to the Scottish people, immediately after the close of the conflict, distinctly declared:—"It is our firm determination ever to maintain that in all questions purely spiritual the judicatures of the Church have the sole right of judging. By these principles we are determined to abide." [41] In more than one notable instance subsequent to 1843, this supremacy of the Church within its own ecclesiastical sphere has been signally recognised by the Civil Courts;[42] and the most illustrious living statesman of Great Britain testified by anticipation that the Church of Scotland was invested, in 1874, through the Act which abolished patronage, with powers not possessed by any other Church in Christendom.[43]

X. The witness of the Scottish Church—of both established and non-established communions—to the principle of spiritual independence, has helped to supply a conspicuous want in Reformed Christendom, and has exerted, doubtless, an appreciable influence beyond

Scotland. Whereas in England, France, Scandinavia, Holland, and Switzerland, the National Reformed Churches have either been from the first, or eventually become, more or less crastian in government and discipline, the Scottish Church has set before Christendom a substantial realisation of Calvin's ideal of a Church at once national and free.

On the one hand, in the Old as well as in the New World, this example of Scotland has, presumably, stimulated the formation and growth of Churches which possess spiritual independence and are without State connection. Both in Great Britain and on the Continent of Europe—notably in Switzerland, Holland, and France—State support has been renounced by a considerable portion of the Protestant populations. This renunciation is due to the conviction that the civil power, in their case, not only encroached upon ecclesiastical jurisdiction, but hindered the conservation or revival of evangelical doctrine, and the diffusion of an earnestly evangelical spirit.[44] In America and in Australia, through combined colonial and religious enterprise, numerous Churches have come into existence which either from the first have been unconnected with the State, or have received from it moderate support without sacrifice of ecclesiastical independence.

On the other hand, there have been notable movements recently in National Churches towards greater freedom of ecclesiastical development and government. In England, the Anglo-Catholic revival, however much to be regretted some of its issues may be, has had, among other commendable results, the restoration of Synodical activity and influence, as well as the deliverance of Church and clergy from phlegmatic acquiescence in an erastian polity. In the National Reformed Church of France, a crave for spiritual freedom and self-government was met by the revival, in 1872, under M. Thiers's Presidency, of the National Synod, through which the voice of the Church, apart from the State, was once more heard. Internal divisions alone appear to have prevented the investment of this Synod with full and supreme legislative authority in the spiritual sphere.[45] In the Evangelical Church of Prussia, and in other German National Churches, the erastian form of ecclesiastical government by royally-appointed Consistories has been, in recent times, so far superseded by a more genuinely Presbyterian constitution, according to which ecclesiastical supervision and discipline are entrusted to congregational Sessions and district Synods, while General Synods are invested with a share of legislative power.[46] It is impossible to doubt that, in some degree, these varied strivings after ecclesiastical autonomy have been encouraged by the example and testimony of a Church whose history, in post-Reformation times, has been characterised by frequent resistance to civil encroachment, and by almost unanimous assertion, amid very varied application, of the principle of spiritual independence.

The testimony of the Scottish Church to the doctrine of spiritual autonomy is still associated, by the majority of the Scottish people, with the maintenance of the principle of Church establishment, and of national responsibility for the provision of religious ordinances throughout the land. The continuance of this twofold testimony is signally important not only for Scotland but for other countries which have national Churches. It means that emphatic witness is borne before Christendom against the practical secularism which would either exclude religion from the sphere of national responsibility, or degrade the Christian Church from a divine institution into a department of State-administration.

To mutilate this combined testimony, through the disestablishment of the existing Church of Scotland, without provision for the establishment in its place of a more comprehensive and therefore more fully national Church, would mean a conspicuous concession to the secular spirit of the time. For it cannot be pleaded that there is, at the present day, any general tendency, of which Church disestablishment might constitute only one among other illustrations, to diminish the area of national responsibility for the welfare of the individual citizen. On the contrary, national accountability has, in recent times, been magnified, instead of being minimised. In our own country, we have illustrations of this direction of public sentiment in the modern Poor Laws, through which the nation, to an extent previously unrealised, has made itself responsible for the decent maintenance of the pauper; and also, more recently, in the Education Acts, through which the State, with an efficiency previously unknown in our country, undertakes to secure the education of every child in the kingdom. We have further illustrations of the same tendency in the growing demand being made, under influential auspices, for national old-age pensions, for public employment of the otherwise unemployed, and for a more complete municipal control, or even actual management, of the traffic on whose careful regulation the repression of intemperance considerably depends. It is impossible, moreover, to ignore the recent growth and diffusion of socialistic opinions which go far beyond such moderate demands in claiming for the individual a public provision. While the duty of the State to promote the material and intellectual well-being of each individual is thus, in various spheres, emphasised and extended, it would be a momentous concession to secularism, if national responsibility for the individual's religious welfare were simultaneously curtailed or practically disowned.

It is possible that in Scotland, at the present time, there is sufficient religious earnestness to undertake the voluntary supply of all the spiritual provision which the population requires, if the national religious endowments were withdrawn from ecclesiastical use. But the removal of buttresses, apparently superfluous, from a building often issues, eventually, in the ruin of the structure. The disavowal, moreover, of national responsibility in one country encourages similar renunciation in others, where less result can be expected from private Christian enterprise; and no voluntary provision of religious ordinances could compensate for the discreditable testimony—pernicious directly to Scotland, and indirectly to Christendom at large—that while the nation, as a nation, provided against any one being starved literally, for lack of food, or intellectually for want of education, men and women were to be allowed, so far as the State was concerned, to starve spiritually for lack of the knowledge which "maketh wise unto salvation."

NOTES

LECTURE I

1. *Rectorial Address* to the students of St. Andrews (1869), p. 9. Cf. Dr. James M'Gregor, in the *Scottish Church* (St. Giles's Lectures), p. 372.

2. "The Bombay merchants are all Scotch. In British settlements from Canada to Ceylon, from Dunedin to Bombay, for every Englishman that you meet who has worked himself up to wealth from small beginnings without external aid, you find ten Scotsmen." Sir Charles Dilke's *Greater Britain*, p. 533.

3. *Confession of St. Patrick* (see below). The earlier reference by Tertullian (in his treatise against the Jews, *circa* 208 A.D.) to "British regions inaccessible to the Romans having been brought under the power of Christ" is significant but vague. It is not likely, however, that, amid the extensive introduction of Roman influences into North Britain after the conquest by Agricola in 80 A.D., the knowledge of Christianity should have been very long withheld.

4. Bede's *Ecclesiastical History*, Book III. chap. iv.

5. See the *Confession of St. Patrick*, generally accepted as genuine on account of combined external and internal evidence. The copy in the Library of Trinity College, Dublin, belongs to the eighth or ninth century, and professes to be transcribed from a document written

by St. Patrick himself. Skene's *Celtic Scotland*, ii. 17 ; G. T. Stokes' *Ireland and the Celtic Church*, p. 26.

6. In the tenth or eleventh century. See Skene's *Chronicles of the Picts and Scots*, Pref. lxxvii.

7. In Iona itself, according to an old Irish Life of Columba, the saint on his arrival found two bishops, whose work he superseded (Skene's *Celtic Scotland*, pp. 34, 491); and it is only reasonable to suppose that a considerable portion of the Scoto-Irish colonists in North Britain after St. Patrick's time were Christians. To this pre-Columban period belongs the legendary history of the Irish St. Buitt, who died in 521, and whose name is preserved in Carbuddo (in Forfarshire). An ancient memoir of him describes his visit to that region and his receiving a grant of land from a King Nectan (Skene's *Chronicles of the Picts and Scots*, p. 410). Among other Irish missionaries who, according to tradition, evangelised districts of North Britain during this period were St. Mochta, who is said to have laboured in the Lennox ; St. Colmoc, who occupied the island called after him, Inchmocholmoc in Lake of Menteith ; and St. Faelan or Fillan (not to be confounded with the later and more famous saint of the same name), who is said to have settled at Dundurn, near Comrie. See Forbes's *Kal. Scot. Sts.* and Stephen's *Scottish Church*, i. p. 35.

8. Cumin, the author of the earlier memoir, became Abbot of Iona in 657, sixty years after Columba died. Adamnan, who incorporated Cumin's biography with his own, was born in 624, twenty-seven years after Columba's death.

9. Adamnan suggests this motive (afterwards distinctly asserted) by associating Columba's departure with the bloody fight of Culdreivny in 561 (see *Memoir*

i. 7 and second preface); but he repudiates by anticipation the later allegation that Columba was forced into missionary exile as an ecclesiastical penance. He records, indeed, an "unjust" excommunication of the saint by a Synod in Meath "for venial reasons," but indicates that the same Synod immediately afterwards recalled the sentence (ii. 4).

10. In an Irish document of the twelfth century, (the *Prophecy* of St. Berchan) the mission of Columba is expressly connected with his concern for the Scots of North Britain, who had been defeated in battle by the Picts three years before, and had been deprived of part of their territory. "Nor was it happy with him (Columba) that an Erinach should be king in the east under the Cruithnigh (Picts)." See Skene's *Chronicles of the Picts and Scots*, p. 82, and his *Celtic Scotland*, vol. ii. pp. 83, 84. "While his missionary zeal impelled him to attempt the conversion of the Picts, he must have felt that if he succeeded in winning a pagan people to the religion of Christ, he would at the same time rescue the Irish colony of Dalriada from a great danger by establishing peaceable relations between them and their greatly more numerous and powerful neighbours."

11. Adam., Second Preface, "Pro Christo peregrinari volens."

12. Bede, B. iii. 4; Adam. i. 8, 24, 25, 27, 39; ii. 20, 47; iii. 15, 20; *Book of Deer*.

13. Reeves's *Adamnan* (in *Historians of Scotland*), Preface, p. lx.

14. Bede, iii. 3.

15. *Ibid.* iii. 5, 26.

16. *Ibid.* iii. 27.

17. *Ibid.* iv. 23. The five bishops were Bosa and

Wilfrid II. of York; Hedda of Dorchester; Oftfor of Worcester, and John of Hexham (John of Beverley).

18. *Life of Wilfrid* by Eddius, chap. 2.
19. Bede, iii. 28.
20. *Ibid.* iii. 22.
21. *Monks of the West* (English translation), iv. p. 88.
22. *Ibid.* iv. pp. 125-127.
23. *Leaders of the Northern Church*, pp. 9, 11, 16.
24. Adam. iii. 24.
25. Skene's *Celtic Scotland*, ii. pp. 80, 81. The tradition is embodied in the work of Manus O'Donnell, compiled in 1532 professedly out of ancient records then extant.
26. Adam. i. 3, 35; ii. 6; Reeves's *Adam.* xlvi.
27. Adam. i. 35, and old Irish Life of Columba (eleventh century) contained in Skene's *Celtic Scotland*, ii. pp. 501, 502. "The kingdom of Dalriada in Scotland was to be freed from all tribute towards the supreme King of Ireland, but they were to join in expeditions and hostings when called upon, with the exception of the sea-gathering." (*Celt. Scot.* ii. 125).
28. Old Irish Life as above, p. 500.
29. Adam. i. 3.
30. *Ibid.* iii. 18.
31. Montalembert, iii. p. 286; Colgan's *Acta Sanctorum*.
32. A list of these is given in Haddan and Stubbs's *Councils and Ecclesiastical Documents*, Vol. II. Part I. pp. 107, 137. The most notable migrations are those of (1) St. Donan, the evangelist of Eig, who, along with fifty companions, suffered martyrdom there in 617, (Forbes's *Kalendar of Scot. Saints*, p. 324); (2) St. Blane (a disciple of Columba's friends Comgall and Kenneth)

who laboured in Bute and is the reputed founder of Dunblane (Skene's *Celt. Scot.* ii. 138); (3) St. Maelrubha, a monk of Bangor, who came over from Ireland in 671, settled in Applecross, and evangelised Ross (Article by Dr. Reeves in *Proceedings of Soc. Ant. Scot.*, 14th June 1859).

33. Neander's *Hist. of Church*, Period III. Sect. I.
34. Colgan's *Acta Sanctorum*, i. 331.
35. Mont. ii. 397; Stokes, pp. 131-148; Fleming's *Collectanea Sacra*.
36. Mont. ii. 460. Gallus is a Latin form of Cellach.
37. Baring-Gould's *Lives of the Saints*, iii. 91.
38. Maclear's *Missions in the Middle Ages*, p. 153.
39. Neander's *History of the Church*, Period III. Sec. I.
40. Mont. iii. 296. Some of these, as that of Ratisbon, lingered on till modern times. See Lecture IV. p. 116.
41. Mont. iii. 256. Among these was the celebrated St. Cathaldus of Munster (Cathal), Bishop of Tarentum in the latter part of the seventh century. Colgan's *Acta Sanctorum*, i. 545.
42. Mont. iii. 250; A. W. Haddan's *Remains*, p. 218. Bangor and Clonard are said to have had at this period 3000 monks each under their jurisdiction.
43. Neander's, Period III. Sect I.
44. *Life of Wilfrid* by Eddius, chap. 26.
45. Bede, v. 19; Eddius, chap. 2.
46. Bede, iv. 9.
47. *Ibid.* iv. 10.
48. Milman's *Latin Christianity*, ii. 114.
49. Bede, i. 25; Stanley's *Memorials of Canterbury*, p. 39.

50. Adam. ii. 3, 46. Even the new church built by Aidan's successor Finan was entirely of wood, thatched with reeds (Bede, iii. 25).

51. Bede, iii. 14.

52. Stanley's *Memorials of Canterbury*, p. 34.

53. Bede, iii. 26.

54. *Ibid.* iii. 4, 17. Bede's prejudice appears even in his reference to Columba himself: "Whatever kind of man he was himself, he left successors, etc."

55. Bede, iii. 3, 5, 17.

56. *Ibid.* iii. 5, 26.

57. Neander, Period III. Sect. I.

58. Boniface is even described as "Scotus natione" (but apparently without authority) by Trithemius in his *De Scriptoribus Eccles.* ccxliv.

59. Embodied in Colgan's *Acta Sanctorum*, vol. i. p. 494. See also O'Hanton's *Lives of Irish Saints*, vol. iii. 183; and Skene's *Chron. Picts and Scots*, pp. xli. 106-116. Colgan endeavours to claim Cadroe for Ireland; but the saint's Scottish birth and parentage are generally admitted, and appear to be fully certified by the references in the ancient biography to his connection with the contemporary Constantine, King of the Scots, and with Donald, King of Strathclyde, as well as by the express statement that Cadroe returned home from Armagh "over the sea."

LECTURE II

1. In 1556 a company of Huguenots and fourteen evangelists from Geneva began missionary work in Brazil; but the enterprise failed through its leader, Villegagnon, becoming a renegade. In 1559, Gustavus

Vasa of Sweden organised a mission to the heathen Lapps under his rule. The colony of Virginia in N.A., founded soon after 1580, had missionary as well as colonising aims, and in 1587 recorded its first Indian baptism. Sir Walter Raleigh gave £100 to the Virginian Company, as a contribution towards the propagation of the Gospel among the pagan natives. See Dr. William Brown's *History of the Propagation of Christianity*, chap. i.; Archdeacon Hardwick's *History of the Reformation*, p. 446.

2. Protestant Holland shared in the commercial enterprise of this period; but its people were engaged in a critical struggle with Spain for civil freedom and religious toleration. Early in the seventeenth century, however, after Dutch independence had been secured, we find a missionary college in Leyden, and organised propagation of the Reformed Faith in the colonies of Java, Formosa, and Ceylon. But the religious intolerance of the Dutch Colonial Government, while it resulted in numerous nominal conversions, was unfavourable to genuine evangelisation. See Brown, i. pp. 10, 22, 25; Dr. George Smith's *Conversion of India*, p. 77.

3. The General Assembly of 1596, in a representation to the King, declares "that in many pairts of the countrie, for lake of sufficient stipends for provisione of pastors, the people lyes altogether ignorant of their salvation and dewtie to God and the King, qwhairthrough the land is overflowit with atheisme and all kynde of vyce, there being above four hundreth paroche kirks destitute of the ministrie of the Word, by and attour the kirks of Argyle and the Isles" (*Book of the Universal Kirk*, p. 437).

4. See *Diary* of James Melville, pp. 433, 434; M'Crie's

Life of Andrew Melville, chap. vii.; Spottiswood's *History*, p. 468.

5. Peterkin's *Records of the Kirk*, vol. i. p. 478. The quotation is an extract from a letter of the General Assembly to the Scots abroad, and the main topic of the letter is the provision of ordinances for them; but a wider missionary scope is here plainly indicated.

6. *Acts of the General Assembly*, 1638-1842; letter of date February 1700.

7. See Howie's *Scots Worthies*, and Dr. Hew Scott's *Fasti*, Part IV. 396. Shields was also the author of *The Hind let Loose* and a *Vindication of our Solemn Covenants*. He was one of the three Cameronian ministers who entered the Church reconstituted in 1690, and he became minister of the second charge at St. Andrews. A brief notice of other ministers who joined the Darien expeditions is contained in the *Fasti*, Part I. p. 400. They belonged chiefly to the sterner section of the post-Revolution clergy (Burton's *Hist. of Scotland*, chap. lxxxv.) Howie suggests that the moderate majority of the Church wished "to get rid" of Shields by sending him out as a missionary to Darien; but more probably he and others of the ten, finding themselves out of sympathy with the "moderation" of the Church, were the more ready to offer themselves for service abroad. Shields died in Jamaica of fever in 1700. A similar fate overtook three (at least) of the others. One (Francis Borland) returned to his parish, Glassford.

8. The Society owed its missionary stimulus mainly to a legacy of Dr. Williams of London, yielding £50 a year and payable "a twelvemonth after the Society have actually sent three missionaries to foreign parts." Communications were opened with the American Presby-

terian Church in 1729, and arrangements were made soon afterwards for the establishment of a mission to the North American Indians; but, owing to various causes of delay, it was not till 1741 that the first missionary, John Sargent, actually entered on his labours among the Indians on the Housatonic. The second, Azariah Horton, began work in the following year on Long Island. See Dr. C. A. Briggs's *American Presbyterianism*, p. 302.

9. Brown's *Propagation of Christianity*, i. pp. 32, 45; Briggs, pp. 97, 98.

10. Jonathan Edwards's *Life of Brainerd*, pp. 307, 308.

11. These were recorded, at the request of the Scottish Society, in his work *Mirabilia Dei inter Indicos*.

12. Brown, i. p. 119.

13. *Missionary Year-Book* of the Religious Tract Society, Section IV. chap. i.

14. Jonathan Edwards's *Life of Brainerd;* Pratt's *Life of Brainerd*, with Bickersteth's Preface; Brown's *Propagation of Christianity*, i. pp. 80-119. David Brainerd was succeeded by his brother John, who died about 1780. Missionary operations were interrupted by the American War of Independence, after which the connection of the Scottish Society with the work ceased.

15. Chap. xxxvii.

16. *Actings and Proceedings* of the General Assembly, 1796. Overtures had been sent from the Synods of Fife and of Moray in favour of a mission being organised by the Assembly.

17. The Moravian Church, or Church of the United Brethren (*Unitas Fratrum*) inaugurated its earliest Foreign Mission in 1732 (to the slaves of St. Thomas Island) under the direction of its General Synod. The

Danish missions in the eighteenth century to the East Indies and to Greenland were organised, not by the Church, but by the Government of Denmark. The Baptist Missionary Society was founded in 1792, not by any representative Council, but by twelve ministers in a private parlour.

18. The "Scottish Missionary Society" was founded in February 1796. Its first missionaries were Henry Brunton and Peter Greig, who were sent to Sierra Leone. The mission came to an untimely end in 1800 in consequence of Mr. Brunton's loss of health and Mr. Greig's murder by a native. The former, along with other labourers, was afterwards sent to Tartary; but the work there, after a promising commencement, had to be abandoned, owing partly to the jealousy of the Greek Church. The Society's more prosperous missions to Bombay and Jamaica were founded in 1822 and 1824 respectively. See Brown's *Propagation of Christianity*, i. pp. 415-49; Dr. Geo. Smith's *Short Hist. of Missions*.

19. The "Glasgow Missionary Society" was also established in February 1796. Its first mission (to West Africa) proved unfortunate and was eventually abandoned; but the mission to the Kaffirs of South Africa, begun in 1821, was a conspicuous success. It included the work of the well-known Lovedale Institution. Brown, i. pp. 450-73.

20. Brown, i. pp. 436, 448, 465.

21. Dr. Love (a native of Paisley), while pastor of Spitalfield Presbyterian Congregation in London, wrote the "first small letter" which called together a few ministers to consult respecting the foundation of the London Society. He remained Secretary until 1800, when he became first minister of Anderston Church,

Glasgow. He was subsequently appointed Secretary of the Glasgow Missionary Society; and it was after him that Lovedale was so called. See *Dict. of National Biography*, vol. xxxiv.; Scott's *Fasti*, Part III.

22. Thomas was originally a surgeon. He was a man of earnest character and varied gifts, although lacking in judgment and stability. He came to England in 1792, and in the following year returned to Bengal as the colleague of Carey. See Brown's *Propagation*, vol. ii. p. 1.

23. "Observations on the State of Society among the Asiatic Subjects of Great Britain."

24. See Dr. George Smith's *Conversion of India*, p. 97; his article on Grant in *Good Words*, Sept. 1891, and his *Life of Alexander Duff*, vol. i. 35, 97. As regards ecclesiastical connection, Dr. Smith describes Grant as "an evangelical Christian first, and a Presbyterian, Baptist, and Episcopalian afterwards, as his position led him."

25. Morrison was born in 1782, and died in 1834. He was a native of Morpeth, but was of Scottish parentage. See Townsend's *Robert Morrison*.

26. Moffat, b. 1795; d. 1883. See *Lives of Robert and Mary Moffat*, by J. S. Moffat.

27. Wilson, b. 1804; d. 1875. See Dr. Geo. Smith's *Life of John Wilson*.

28. Paton, b. 1824. See *Autobiography* edited by his brother.

29. Macfarlane, b. 1840; d. 1887. See Kilgour's *Darjeeling Mission* (in the press).

30. Mackay, b. 1849; d. 1890. See *Memoir* by his sister.

31. Morrison and Moffat were Congregationalists; Wilson belonged to the Church of Scotland, and afterwards to the Free Church; Paton was sent out by

the Reformed Presbyterian Church; Macfarlane was a missionary of the Church of Scotland; Mackay (son of a Free Church minister) was an Episcopal missionary under the C.M.S.

32. Inglis succeeded Principal Robertson as minister of Old Greyfriars Church, Edinburgh. He was a prominent leader of the "Moderates," but was highly esteemed by all parties. The writer remembers hearing a warm tribute paid to his memory and work by the late Dr. Guthrie from the Moderator's Chair of the Free Church General Assembly in 1862 or 1863. In his opening address as Moderator of that Assembly in 1896, Principal Miller of Madras spoke of the "sanctified statesmanship of Dr. Inglis" finding "its fitting instrument in the evangelical fervour of Dr. Duff." Unhappily for the Church of Scotland, Dr. Inglis died early in 1834, before the "Ten Years' Conflict" began. His son was Lord President of the Court of Session from 1867 to 1891.

33. Duff's *India and India Missions*, p. 481. "Of this rudimental scheme the sole, the undisputed author was Dr. Inglis. With him it originated as the product of his own solitary independent reflection on the known constitution of the human mind and the general history of man."

34. Duff's *India and India Missions*, p. 485. Dr. Inglis and other influential leaders of the Church were strongly supported in their advocacy of an India Mission by Dr. Bryce, the first Chaplain of the Church of Scotland at Calcutta. Dr. Bryce's proposals, however, differed notably from Dr. Inglis's scheme, and aimed at reaching the better-informed and influential natives by means of lectures and addresses on the doctrines and evidences of

Christianity, to be delivered by the missionaries in the vernacular tongues. See Dr. Niven's reference in Story's *Church of Scotland*, iii. p. 766; and *Special Report of Foreign Mission Committee* to General Assembly of Church of Scotland, pp. 295, 296.

35. Christian Friedrich Schwarz, a native of Brandenburg, laboured in India from 1750 until his death in 1798. William Carey's missionary career extended from 1793 till 1834.

36. Smith's *Life of Duff*, vol. i. pp. 103, 116, 144.

37. Letter of Dr. Duff in Smith's *Life*, vol. i. p. 172. In 1830 the total number of Indian native Christians baptized under Protestant auspices was only 27,000. See Smith's *Conversion of India*, p. 137. The number in 1890 was 648,800 (Smith, p. 204), and is estimated as now nearly a million.

38. Carey's establishment included not only a "Normal department to train native teachers" and a "Theological Institute to equip the Eurasian and native Christian students, by a quite unsectarian course of study, to be missionaries to the Brahminical classes," but a curriculum of study in "the English language and literature," to enable the senior students (without distinction) "to dive into the deepest recesses of European science." Unfortunately, however, the Serampore College lost all the funds it possessed in India owing to a financial collapse in Bengal during 1830-33; Carey's own personal income was simultaneously cut down; and the educational department of the Serampore Mission failed to secure adequate appreciation at home. See Smith's *Life of Carey*, pp. 381, 382.

39. "It was founded originally for a Principal and two Professors, and as many students as its funds

should enable the Society to maintain during the period of study, and to provide for afterwards in the situations of missionaries, schoolmasters, and catechists at its various stations. These stations were to be under episcopal jurisdiction. As the object of the institution was expressly the propagation of the Gospel, no students were to be admitted who should not propose to devote themselves to that object." Le Bas's *Life of Bishop Middleton*, ii. p. 107. It is true that a secondary object of the institution was to teach "the elements of useful knowledge and the English language" to "native children without any immediate view to their becoming Christians" (Le Bas, ii. 18, 20), but this could not meet the need of the time. The building is now a Government Engineering College.

40. Duff's *India Missions*, pp. 520-22.
41. Smith's *Life of Duff*, vol. i. pp. 105, 106.
42. Duff's *India Missions*, pp. 507, 525-29.
43. *Ibid.* p. 519. The new movement was stigmatised by the Orientalists as "Anglomania." It is to be kept in mind that the Scottish Missionaries did not ultroneously substitute Western for Oriental culture; but, finding the former already in favour, they endeavoured to Christianise it.
44. Smith's *Life of Duff*, vol. i. p. 141.
45. *Ibid.* vol. i. pp. 167, 207.
46. *Ibid.* vol. i. 159-63, 470-75; vol. ii. 53, 54, 78. "Dr. Duff's converts are the backbone of the native Church in Bengal" (Rev. A. Clifford, Secretary of Church Missionary Society, Calcutta, in *Special Report* of Church of Scotland Foreign Mission Committee on Educational Missions, 1890).
47. See *Special Report* above mentioned, and *Mission-*

ary *Year-Book* of Religious Tract Society. Principal Miller of Madras, in his Opening Address as Moderator of the Free Church General Assembly (1896) declares (p. 20) that "the scheme of Christian education in India is the most original and influential contribution we have made to the carrying of Gospel light to the lands that sit in darkness. For, be it remembered that every section of the Church at work in India, not those alone that are of our kin, but that part of England's Church to which Protestant is a distasteful word, and the organisations also that are in obedience to Rome, have followed the example which Scotland set." Dr. Pierson bears eloquent testimony to Dr. Duff's potent influence upon American Missions in his *New Acts of the Apostles*, p. 130.

48. Smith's *Life of Duff*, chap. vii.; Principal Morrison in *Special Report* of Foreign Mission Committee, p. 292.

49. Smith's *Life of Duff*, vol. ii. p. 394.

50. Letter from Sir Charles Trevelyan to Dr. George Smith after Dr. Duff's death. See Smith's *Life of Duff*, vol. i. 195, 196.

51. The oldest organisation specifically for Medical Missions is the Edinburgh Medical Missionary Society, constituted in 1841. Besides maintaining agencies of its own, it supplies Medical Missionaries to most of the larger Missionary Societies.

52. Six years ago the Church of Scotland Foreign Mission Committee received (in answer to request) opinions on this subject from eight-four representative Anglo-Indians of high position, belonging to various spheres of public service. Of these sixty-eight were distinctly, and in most cases warmly, favourable to

Mary, and Elizabeth (whose legitimacy was disputed), heir to the English throne. An eventual marriage between Edward and Mary was, during their infancy, part of Henry VIII.'s policy, with a view to the union of the crowns, and was agreed to by the Scottish Estates in 1543. During the Reformation struggle in Scotland the Scottish Protestant party, or a section of it, was in more or less open alliance with Henry VIII., Protector Somerset, and Elizabeth successively.

2. Froude's *History of England*, vi. 511 (cabinet ed.); Burton's *History of Scotland*, iv. 64-66 (ed. 1876).

3. Froude, vii. 177; viii. 272; ix. 125-27.

4. *Ibid.* vi. 573; Paton's *British History and Papal Claims*, i. 100-102; Stephen's *Scottish Church*, ii. 117.

5. Froude, vi. 449; vii. 368; Burton, iv. 131-35; Paton, pp. 104, 107, 108; Letters of Mary Stewart in Labanoff's Collection, i. pp. 175-77, 179, 281, 355, 369; ii. 7; vii. 6-10; Bellesheim's *Catholic Church of Scotland*, iii. 93, 94; Moncrieff's *Influence of Knox and the Scottish Reformation on England* (Exeter Hall Lectures, 1859-60), p. 32.

The League included the Pope (Pius V.), the Emperor, the Kings of Spain and Portugal, the Dukes of Bavaria and Savoy, and the Republic of Venice. The English ambassador, Randolph, asserts that Mary Stewart signed the "band." This is a disputed point; but, as Burton remarks, "whether in the form of a band or not, beyond doubt Mary was the close ally of the King of Spain in all his formidable views and projects for crushing the new religion."

6. Moncrieff, pp. 33-36; Laing's *John Knox*, ii. 139, 146, 554; Hume Brown's *John Knox*, ii. 291; Froude, vii. 90, 91; ix. 243; in *Short Sketches*, i. 114, he ascribes to Knox the prevention of a Spanish invasion in 1571.

7. Seton was Confessor to James V. in that king's youth, and afterwards became chaplain to the Duke of Suffolk, brother-in-law of Henry VIII. M'Alpine was Prior of the Dominican Convent at Perth from 1532 until his flight in 1534. He was presented by Shaxton, the first Protestant Bishop of Salisbury, to a canonry in 1538. Subsequently he rendered conspicuous service to the Reformation cause in Denmark (see Lecture IV. p. 115, and note 15). M'Dowel was sub-Prior of the Blackfriars' Monastery in Glasgow, became chaplain to the Bishop of Salisbury, and was the first in that cathedral to assail publicly the doctrine of Papal Supremacy. See Lorimer's *Patrick Hamilton*, pp. 181-87.

8. Hume Brown's *John Knox*, i. p. 104; Laing's *Works of Knox*, vi. 26, where an extract is given from the Record Office in London of eighty "persons that have had licence to preach under the ecclesiastical seal since July 1547."

Rough, originally a Dominican Prior at Stirling, was one of the Earl of Arran's Reforming Chaplains in 1543, and afterwards preacher to the garrison in the Castle of St. Andrews after the assassination of Cardinal Beaton. It was through Rough that John Knox was called by the congregation of the Castle to the ministry. He suffered martyrdom at Smithfield in 1557 under Mary Tudor (M'Crie's *Life of Knox*, Period ii.; Lorimer's *Precursors of Knox*, p. 188). Willock, originally a Dominican in Ayrshire, became, after his return from England, one of Knox's coadjutors in Scotland, and was "Superintendent of the West" in the Reformed Church. Even before he was appointed to that office, the Reformers of Ayrshire called him the "Primate" (Laing's *Knox*, i. 245; M'Crie's *Knox*, Per. iv. and vi.; Lorimer's *Precursors*, 190, 191). John M'Brair was a gentleman of Galloway, who fled to England in 1538 to escape persecution at home. He afterwards preached to the English congregation at Frankfort, and eventually became a vicar in Newcastle (M'Crie's *Knox*, note 1).

In addition to the foregoing we find in the Record Office list the names of John Blythe, "Scottishman, Master of Arts," and Thomas Gilham, "Scottishman, Bachelor of Divinity." Among Scotsmen who were preachers in England during the same period, without the special licence of the Government, was William Harlaw, afterwards minister of St. Cuthbert's, Edinburgh (1560-78).

9. Laing's *Knox*, ii. 278.

10. M'Crie's *Knox*, Per. ii.; Lorimer's *John Knox and the Church of England*, chap. i.; Laing's *Knox*, ii. 280. Addressing Mary on one occasion, Knox declared that "God so blessed my weak labours that in Berwick, while commonly before there used to be slaughter by reason of quarrels that used to arise among soldiers, there was as great quietness all the time that I remained there as there is this day in Edinburgh."

11. The "Council of the North" consisted of the leading nobility and gentry of the North of England, and was nominated by the Government for the administration of public and ecclesiastical affairs. Knox's address on the occasion is given by Laing, vol. iii. 32.

12. Laing's *Knox*, iii. pp. 81, etc.; Tytler's *England under Edward VI. and Mary*, ii. 142, 148; Hume Brown's *Knox*, i. 122. Northumberland wished to strengthen the cause of the Reformation in the South

of England; and the presence of Knox, who discerned his selfish character and reproved his vices, had become disagreeable.

13. The fact of Knox's chaplaincy has been called in question; but his autograph signature, among those of the other five chaplains, is extant, appended to the Forty-five Articles (afterwards Forty-two), and dated October 1552 (Laing's *Knox*, vi. 29, 30).

14. "Kneeling at the Lord's Supper I thought good amongst you to avoid, and to use sitting at the Lord's Table, which ye did not refuse" (Letter of Knox to the congregation of Berwick, a year or two after he had left them. Lorimer's *John Knox and the Church of England*, p. 261). In 1550 Bishop Hooper advocated the same posture; and in the reign of Mary, Thomas Becon, who had been Cranmer's chaplain, writes in his *Displaying of the Popish Mass*, "Oh, how oft have I seen here in England, at the ministration of Holy Communion, people sitting at the Lord's Table." A letter from John Utenhove to Bullinger (in 1552) indicates a sermon by a Scotsman (referring doubtless to Knox) as the chief occasion of the movement against kneeling (Drysdale's *History of the Presbyterians in England*, p. 66).

A memorial to the Privy Council, of date 1552 (discovered by Dr. Lorimer), in favour of sitting at Communion is proved by internal and external evidence to have been substantially the work of Knox. The objection to kneeling was not sustained by the Council, but the memorial led to the adoption, as a compromise, of the "Black Rubric," which was a virtual concession to the views of Knox and of those who sympathised with him (Lorimer's *Knox*, p. 275).

15. That contemporaries attributed the insertion of

the Rubric to Knox's influence and representations, appears from a reference in Foxe's *Acts and Monuments* (vi. 510) to a disputation between Latimer and Dean Weston (1554), in which the latter says, "A runagate Scot did take away the adoration of Christ in the Sacrament, by whose procurement that heresy was put into the last Communion Book; so much prevailed that one man's authority at that time." The "runagate Scot" is generally admitted to be Knox. See Laing's *Knox*, iii. 80; Hume Brown's *Knox*, i. 132; Drysdale's *Presbyterians in England*, p. 68.

16. See Lorimer's *Knox*, p. 125; Hume Brown, i. 130. The alteration due directly to Knox's intervention was the significant omission of a clause endorsing the ceremonies of the Prayer-Book as "in no point repugnant to the wholesome doctrine of the Gospel."

17. Laing's *Knox*, iii. 360, 365, 374; Hume Brown, i. 143, 144.

18. Besides writings which are lost, there remain (1) "A Godly Letter of Warning or Admonition to the Faithful in London, Newcastle, and Berwick" (1554); (2) two "Comfortable Epistles to his afflicted Brethren in England" (1554); (3) "A Faithful Admonition to the Professors of God's Truth in England" (1554); (4) "An Epistle to the Inhabitants of Newcastle and Berwick" (1558). See Drysdale, p. 66.

19. Knox was summoned from Geneva in the autumn of 1554 to the pastorate of the Frankfort congregation; and Thomas Lever was afterwards appointed as his colleague. In March 1555 he withdrew for the sake of peace, mainly on account of difficulties which arose in the congregation over the question of the liturgy to be used. In the autumn of 1555, during his prolonged

visit to Scotland, he was appointed pastor of the newly formed English congregation at Geneva, with Christopher Goodman as colleague. His connection with that congregation was not finally severed until the spring of 1559, when he returned to Scotland to take part in the closing struggle which issued in the Scottish Reformation. See Lorimer, pp. 201-44; Hume Brown, i. pp. 162-214.

Whittingham was the chief author of the Geneva Translation of the Bible; Gilby and Sampson were his leading coadjutors. Whittingham afterwards became Dean of Durham. Foxe was the famous Martyrologist. Coverdale, the translator of the English Bible of 1535, had been Bishop of Exeter under Edward VI. John Cole became Archdeacon of Exeter under Elizabeth. Sampson refused the See of Norwich in the same reign because of his Puritan convictions, and was afterwards imprisoned for nonconformity.

20. The full title is "Brief Exhortation to England for the speedy entrance of Christ's Gospel, heretofore by the tyranny of Mary suppressed and banished." See Laing's *Knox*, v. 495-522; Lorimer's *Knox*, p. 214. In this manifesto the Reformer proposes the subdivision of each diocese into ten districts, each district to be under a bishop or superintendent; and he sketches a programme of educational reform, the leading feature of which is the erection of higher schools in all divisions "for the preservation of religion as well as the diffusion of education."

21. Carlyle, *On Heroes, Hero-worship, and the Heroic in History*, p. 133.

22. Calderwood's *History of the Kirk of Scotland*, ii. p. 332; Lorimer's *Knox*, p. 225. This letter is signed by

Craig, Pont, Wynrame, James Melville, Row, Spottiswood, and other Scottish Church leaders. Knox's name is not appended, probably because he was not a *persona grata* with some of the English bishops, on account of his pronounced Puritanism; but it is significant that at the Assembly which sent the letter he obtained six months' leave of absence, which he spent in England, and which he occupied partly, doubtless, as Dr. Lorimer suggests, in communication with English Puritans.

23. Drysdale, pp. 105, 124, 143, 161; Lorimer's *Knox*, p. 235. The leader of the English Puritans, Thomas Cartwright, printed in 1577 his work on Church Discipline in Scotland.

24. Row, in his *History of the Kirk* (p. 220), indicates the hopes then entertained in Scotland of England being "reduced to Presbyterial government." In 1592 the King had taken an active part in the establishment of Presbyterianism; and in 1590 he is said to have uttered the famous dictum about the Liturgy of the Church of England being "an evil said mass in English" (Scot's *Apol. Narr.* p. 57). The Millenary petition of 1603 was so called not because it was signed by 1000 persons, the actual number being 750, but because it refers to a thousand clergy of the Church groaning under grievances which the petitioners sought to have removed. The document is entitled "The humble petition of the ministers of the Church of England desiring reformation of certain ceremonies and abuses of the Church." The grievances complained of related to matters of ritual, discipline, and doctrine, and did not touch the question of episcopal government. Other petitions, however, less numerously

signed, were presented to James about the same time, craving for "presbyterial consent and council in Church affairs." See Drysdale, p. 235. The Puritan crave received nominal consideration but real disregard at the Hampton Court Conference in 1604.

25. According to the sentence passed on Leighton by the Star Chamber, he was to be imprisoned for life and fined £10,000 ; to be publicly whipped and put in the pillory ; to have his nose slit and one of his ears cut off; and to have his face branded with S.S. (Sower of Sedition). He himself, in his *Brief Discoverie*, published in 1646, testifies to the infliction of the foregoing physical mutilation and torture. He was liberated by the Long Parliament in 1641, after ten years' imprisonment ; reparation was ordered to be made "for his great sufferings and damages." See Irving's *Scottish Writers*, ii. pp. 114-20 ; Drysdale, pp. 248-52 ; Rushworth's *Historical Collections*, vol. i. Part III. 228, 229.

26. The negotiations referred to were those which issued in the royal ratification of the abolition of Episcopacy in Scotland. The Scottish Commissioners included Henderson, Gillespie, and Baillie, who preached every Sunday in London to overflowing congregations on the points in controversy between Puritans and Prelatists. Among other controversial pamphlets issued at this period were Henderson's "Unlawfulness and Danger of Limited Prelacy or Perpetual Presidency," a treatise with a similar title by Baillie, and Gillespie's "Grounds of Presbyterial Government." See Cunningham's *Church of Scotland*, chap. xvii. ; Drysdale, p. 269 ; Clarendon's *History of the Rebellion*, i. 151. "To hear those sermons there was so great conflux and resort by the citizens, that from the first appearance of day on

every Sunday to the shutting in of the light the Church was never empty " (Clar.)

27. Cunningham, ii. 44 (2nd ed.); Drysdale, pp. 283, 291; Dr. James Kerr's *The Covenants and the Covenanters*, pp. 141, 151, 173, 212, 237, 277, 307, 310, 311.

28. Drysdale, pp. 553, 572; Howie's *Scots Worthies*, William Veitch and Alexander Peden.

29. In 1717, two Presbyterian ministers of Exeter, Peirce and Hallet, were extruded for Arianism; but in 1719, at the Salters' Hall Synod in London, a resolution against the imposition of any subscription was carried by a small majority, and the Arian leaven spread. In 1733, Strong of Ilminster issued an Arian version of the Shorter Catechism; and, three years later, the revision was re-issued by Samuel Brown of Birmingham, with recommendations by six other leading Presbyterian ministers. About the same time, Pelagianism was advanced by Dr. John Taylor of Norwich. Somewhat later Dr. Joseph Priestley, who had previously surrendered the doctrines of the Trinity and the Atonement, became the leader of an aggressive Socinian movement. His chief works in this connection were his *History of the Conceptions of Christianity* (1782), and his *History of Opinions concerning the Person of Jesus Christ* (1786). See Drysdale, pp. 499-532.

30. The most notable Scottish divine charged with Arian or semi-Arian views was Professor Simson of Glasgow, who, after long controversy, was in 1729 suspended (permanently) from teaching (see Lecture V. note 56).

31. Drysdale, pp. 551-60; John Black's *Presbyterianism in England*, pp. 10, 11. Among notable Scottish

ministers in London during this period were Dr. William Wishart, eventually Principal of Edinburgh University; and Dr. Henry Hunter, a popular evangelical preacher, translated from a Scottish parish in 1771, and for many years the leader of the "Scots Presbytery." In Stafford a minister of the Church of Scotland, Henry Proctor, who settled there in 1789, notably strengthened the cause of orthodox and evangelical Puritanism (Drysdale, p. 564).

32. An old MS., preserved by the Presbyterians of Harbottle in Northumberland, referring to the period between 1736 and 1760, records the frequent participation by ministers of the Church of Scotland in the Communion services held in that county; and also the observance of Scottish Sacramental usages, including the Monday Thanksgiving. See Black, p. 23.

33. Richmond's *Protestant Nonconformity in Stockton*, quoted by Drysdale, p. 551. The writer of the letter quoted in the text was the Rev. William Wood. To the same effect Dr. Priestley in his *Free Address to Protestant Dissenters* (1769), referring to "vacancies supplied from Scotland," adds significantly, "How they are supplied from this quarter let the state of the dissenting interest in the North of England testify" (Drysdale, p. 552). In the middle and latter part of the eighteenth century, the zeal of the newly-founded Scottish Secession operated in the same direction of strengthening the anti-Arian and anti-Socinian party; for the Seceders sent, among other less noted divines, the celebrated John Brown of Haddington on preaching tours throughout the North of England. Not a few Presbyterian congregations were then planted, which afterwards grew into an important organisation.

34. See Drysdale, pp. 605-12; and Black, p. 20, where it is stated that seventy English congregations "formed themselves between 1836 and 1842 into an English Synod in ecclesiastical communion with the Church of Scotland." In 1843 they took the side of the Free Church. Another section of English Presbyterians had previously incorporated themselves with one or other of the Scottish Secession Churches which in 1847 became the U.P. Church. In 1876 this corporate union was dissolved, and the two English sections united under the name of the Presbyterian Church of England, which now numbers about 400 congregations.

35. See Bishop Warburton's Letter in Sir H. Moncreiff Wellwood's *Life of Erskine*, p. 47. "Every branch of science flourishes in the north better than in the south." For the appreciation of Beattie's *Essay on Truth* in England see Forbes's *Life of Beattie*, i. 227, 264. "In England," wrote Bishop Porteous to Dr. Beattie in 1772, "your book has been received with unanimous applause." "The backbone of British theology and religion," wrote Dean Stanley (*Edin. Rev.* April 1881), "is, in a great degree, to be found in the rational and comprehensive faith, at once vigorous and Christian, which characterises the leading spirits of the Church of Scotland at this moment: Principal Caird, whose lectures (on the Philosophy of Religion) we reviewed in our last number; Norman Macleod, but lately removed, too early for his Church and country; Principal Tulloch, whose work on the *Rational Theology of England* is at once an example and a light to be followed." See also Stanley's *Church of Scotland*, pp. 173, 174. Dr. Milligan's *Resurrection of our Lord* is prescribed to candidates for ordination in several

English dioceses, and is also used (in a translation) by the Greek Church.

36. Routh dedicated his *Reliquiae Sacrae* in 1814, "Patribus in Christo admodum reverendis, virisque optimis ac venerabilibus, episcopis et presbyteris Ecclesiae Scoticae Episcopalis, doctis, piis, orthodoxis." Bishop Skinner's *Primitive Truth and Order*, published in 1803, was declared by clergymen of the Church of England to have rendered "very essential service" to that Church, and to have placed it "under infinite obligations." John Skinner's (jun.) *Annals of Scottish Episcopacy*, pp. 320, 322. Bishop Jolly (1756-1838) was accustomed to read the Greek and Latin Fathers, especially Chrysostom and Augustine, daily from 4 a.m. to breakfast time. In an earlier generation Bishop Sage of Edinburgh had set an example of patristic learning by his work on the "Principles of the Cyprianic Age"; Bishops Falconer and Gadderar had contended for the revival of primitive "usages"; and Rattray, Bishop of Dunkeld (d. 1743), had led the way in liturgical studies through his critical edition of the "Ancient Liturgy of the Church of Jerusalem." See Keith's *Catalogue of Scottish Bishops*, Russel's Appendix; Stephen's *Scottish Church*, ii. 456, 491, 511, 556, 603. The late Bishop Wordsworth of St. Andrews, in his *Annals of my Life* (ii. 62), referring to the Oxford Movement, writes: "The more the leaders were discountenanced by authorities in England, the more they looked to our Scotch Church as the soil in which they might still hope to see the growth of their opinions and the success of their cause." See also Stephen, ii. p. 600.

37. See Lecture V. p. 138, and note 7.

38. Stephen's *Scottish Church*, ii. pp. 582, 583.

39. Bishop Samuel Wilberforce, to whose efforts and influence the re-establishment of Convocation in 1852, with Synodical powers, was mainly due, took a deep interest in Scottish ecclesiastical history and affairs; and it is significant that he visited Scotland in the autumn preceding the agitation for the revival of Convocation. See *Life of Wilberforce*, ii. 136-56; iii. 68, 69, 243, 302, 303, 336, 353, 381. In several English dioceses there is a Sustentation Fund for the support of clergy. Both the name and its application are borrowed from the financial system of the Scottish Episcopal Church and of the Free Church of Scotland, in which the term Sustentation Fund originated.

40. Southey's *Life of Wesley*, ii. 246.

41. Samuel Bradburn's *Are the Methodists Dissenters?* quoted by Drysdale, p. 552.

42. Samuel Wesley, the father of the Methodist leaders, eventually Rector of Epworth in Lincolnshire, was educated at Dissenting Academies near London (George Smith's *Wesleyan Methodism*, i. 75). The maternal grandfather of the Wesleys was Dr. Samuel Annesley, their maternal great-grandfather John White of Dorchester (Smith, i. 82, 83).

43. See *Are the Methodists Dissenters?* quoted by Drysdale, p. 592.

44. Alexander Kilham (1762-98) became, after John Wesley's death in 1791, an influential leader of Methodism, and was Superintendent at Aberdeen from 1792-95. He wrote strongly-worded pamphlets against what he regarded as the "hierarchism" of the Methodist constitution, and was expelled from the connection in 1796. A resolution of the Conference at Leeds in 1797, definitely deciding against the admission of lay

representatives either to its own meetings or to a second house of legislation, led to the secession of several pastors, who along with Kilham founded the New Connexion. See George Smith's *Wesleyan Methodism*, vol. ii. pp. 35-144; and *Dict. Nat. Biog.* xxxi. 103.

45. Skene's *Celtic Scotland*, ii. p. 30; Forbes's *Kal. Scot. Saints*, pp. 450, 451; and his *Missale de Arbuthnott*, lxxxiv.; (in accordance with early Irish documents).

46. Skene, ii. p. 489; Forbes's *St. Ninian and St. Kentigern*, xlii. xliii.

47. See Lecture I. note 7.

48. Skene's *Celtic Scotland*, ii. chap. vi.

49. Killen's *Ecclesiastical History of Ireland*, ii. pp. 546-48; and Hamilton's *Irish Presbyterian Church*, pp. 31, 189, 190, in which some notable statistics are adduced. Ulster pays nearly one-half of the Income Tax collected in Ireland under Schedule D. Less than half the number of police in proportion to population are needed for Ulster than are required for Ireland as a whole. Only about one-tenth of the troops in Ireland are quartered in this province. In 1895 only one person in ninety-seven received parochial relief in Ulster, while in the other provinces, taken together, the proportion was one in thirty-nine.

50. Shortly before this greater plantation, through which the best portions of Londonderry, Donegal, Tyrone, Cavan, Armagh, and Fermanagh were allocated by the Crown to British colonists, a similar plantation on a smaller scale had been accomplished by private arrangement in Down and Antrim, Scots from Ayrshire taking the chief part in the enterprise. See Harrison's *Scot in Ulster*, pp. 10, 18, 25, 36, 39.

51. Heylin's *History of Presbyterians*, pp. 387, 388.

"The plantation was carried on more vigorously by adventurers of the Scottish nation, who procured themselves into this country as the richer soil." See also Harrison, pp. 40, 41, 104, 105; Reid's *Presbyterian Church in Ireland*, i. pp. 80-90; Killen, pp. 482-85.

52. Du Pin (R.C.), in his *Eccles. History of the Seventeenth Century* (Book iv. chap. vii.), comparing Ulster with other parts of Ireland at this period, declares that the former was "the most constant in preserving the Catholic religion," whereas "in the other provinces heresy made great progress, and the Catholic religion was almost banished in some places." Reid states that "the sees of Derry, Raphoe, and Clogher, which comprised the greater part of the province, were occupied so late as 1605 by Roman Catholic prelates."

53. In 1610 Derry and Clogher were occupied by George Montgomery, a Scot; Raphoe by Andrew Knox, a kinsman of the Reformer; Down and Connor by James Dundas, also a Scot, whose two successors, Echlin (1612) and Leslie (1636), were of the same nationality. See Killen, i. 489, 490.

54. Walter Travers, an English Presbyterian, who had been inhibited from preaching in England by Primate Whitgift, was Provost of Trinity College, Dublin, in the reign of Elizabeth; and two of the Fellows, Fullerton and Hamilton (under whom Archbishop Ussher received his early training), were Scottish Presbyterians. See Killen, i. p. 453. No regular Presbyterian congregations, however, appear to have been formed.

55. See Lecky's *England in the Eighteenth Century*, ii. p. 109, and Reid's *Presbyterian Church in Ireland*, i. 96-98, in which contemporary testimony is quoted. The son of

one of the ministers who came over from Scotland (Stewart of Donegore) declares that "most of the people were void of godliness, who seemed rather to flee from God in this enterprise than to follow their own mercy ; yet God followed them." . . . "A band of faithful ministers were now engaged to take their lot in Ulster, whose labours were remarkably blest to the converting of many out of so profane and godless a multitude." Robert Blair (*Life*, p. 51) testifies that "although amongst those whom divine Providence did send to Ireland there were several persons eminent for birth, education, and parts ; yet the most were such as either poverty, scandalous lives, or, at the best, adventurous seeking of better accommodation, had forced thither." It is possible, however, that the desire to emphasise the improvement which took place in the lives of the colonists may have led to some exaggeration in the description of their original character. See Harrison, p. 56.

56. Edward Brice (in Scotland Bryce), a native of Airth in Stirlingshire, who had resisted Spottiswood's appointment as permanent Moderator of the Synod of Clydesdale, was deposed by the Presbytery of Glasgow in 1613 for alleged, but unproved, immorality. He came to Antrim in the same year. His younger contemporary Livingstone describes him as "insisting most on the life of Christ in the heart, and on the light of His Word and Spirit in the mind." He died in Ireland in 1636. See his *Life*, p. 78 ; Reid, i. 98 ; Hamilton, pp. 36, 37.

57. Robert Cunningham, who had been chaplain to the Earl of Buccleuch's Regiment in Holland, was admitted to the cure of Holywood in 1615. Ejected

for nonconformity in 1636, he came to Ayrshire, and died at Irvine in 1637. See Reid, i. 206, 207.

58. Robert Blair, a native of Irvine, was Regent in the University of Glasgow during the principalship of Cameron (see Lecture IV. note 20), whose ecclesiastical policy he opposed. He came to Ireland in 1623; was ejected for nonconformity in 1635; returned to Scotland in 1637, and in the following year was appointed to St. Andrews. He visited Ulster in 1642, during the Rebellion, but returned to his charge in Scotland. He was ejected after the Restoration, and died at Aberdeen in 1666. See Howie's *Scots Worthies*.

59. Welsh was Professor of Humanity in Glasgow, but resigned his Chair in 1626. "A great measure of that spirit," testifies Blair, "which wrought in and by the father, rested on the son." He died in 1634. See Reid, i. 112, 178, 179; Howie's *Scots Worthies*.

60. James Hamilton had been educated for the ministry in Scotland, but acted as steward to his uncle, Viscount Claneboye (who had received a large grant of land in 1605), until Blair and Cunningham "being satisfied with his gifts," procured his ordination and appointment to the cure of Ballywalter. He was deposed in 1636 for nonconformity to the new Episcopal Canons, and afterwards became minister of Dumfries. He was one of the Commissioners appointed in 1644 to administer the Solemn League and Covenant in Ulster. At the Restoration he was ejected from his charge in Edinburgh, to which he had been translated from Dumfries. He died in 1666. See Reid, i. 104, ii. 27-42; and *Dict. Nat. Biog.*

61. George Dunbar came to Ireland about 1628, and ministered successively at Carrickfergus and Ballymena,

prior to his settlement at Larne. After his deposition for nonconformity, he returned to Scotland and became minister of Calder. He died in 1641. Reid, i. 113, 114, 221.

62. John Livingstone was the chief instrument of the famous Shotts revival (June 1630), at which the Thanksgiving Service on the Monday after the Communion is said to have originated. He came to Ulster in the autumn of 1630, and laboured there until his deprivation in 1636. He afterwards became minister successively of Stranraer and Ancrum, and took part in the Glasgow Assembly of 1639. He often revisited Ulster after his return to Scotland. During the Commonwealth he joined the "Protesters," and was their Moderator in 1651. After the Restoration he was banished, and settled in Rotterdam, where he died in 1672. His linguistic scholarship was conspicuous. See *Scots Worthies*, and Dr. Sprott's article in the *Dict. Nat. Biog.*

63. Brice, Cunningham, Blair, Hamilton, Welsh, and Livingstone were all admitted to parishes in Ireland by bishops (Reid, i. 99, 101, 103, 104, 112, 116). When Blair was to be settled in Bangor, he intimated to Echlin, Bishop of Down, that he could not accept Episcopal ordination; whereupon Echlin considerately arranged that he should be ordained by Cunningham and other Presbyters in association with the Bishop, who declared that "he took part in the ordination in no other relation than as a Presbyter" (Killen, i. 426). The introduction, however, of the "Hundred Episcopal Canons" in 1634 led to the deprivation of the leading Presbyterian ministers (Reid, i. 188-200; Killen, ii. 24).

64. Clogy, a contemporary Anglo-Irish writer,

declares that "the Irish hatred was greater against the English nation than against their religion." Referring to "the English and Scotch Papists that were fled into Ireland," he declares that "the wrath of God fell upon them also, as well as upon the Protestants," and that the "bloody two-handed sword made no difference" between a Catholic and a heretic (*Life of Bedell*, pp. 174, 175). The rebel leaders appear at first to have endeavoured to exempt the Scotch from the general massacre, and the English suffered most as the direct representatives of "foreign" conquest; but the distinction could not be maintained (Lecky, ii. 130).

65. Clarendon's estimate was 40,000 or 50,000 (*History of Rebellion*, i. 229). Carte, after mentioning exaggerated estimates, agrees with Sir William Petty (who was contemporary with the massacre) that the number killed in the first year of the "troubles" was about 37,000. But Warner (middle of the eighteenth century), basing his calculations on depositions in the library of Trinity College, Dublin, estimates the total as 4000 massacred, and 8000 killed through ill-usage (*History of Rebellion*, ii. 9). Lecky inclines to Warner's estimate (*England in the Eighteenth Century*, ii. 169); Reid (i. 336, 337) and Killen (ii. 38, 39) to that of Petty and Carte.

66. See Burton's *History of Scotland*, chap. lxxiii.; Reid, i. 304, 351; ii. 57; Killen, ii. 52.

67. Reid, i. 368-85; Killen, ii. 53. Among the deputies were the formerly ejected Robert Blair, James Hamilton, and John Livingstone.

68. Adair's *True Narrative*, pp. 103, 104, 214, 215; Reid, ii. 26-44; Killen, ii. 54, 55, 107. The leading Commissioner was James Hamilton, formerly of Ballywalter.

69. According to Sir W. Petty (*Political Survey of*

Ireland, published in 1719), a large fresh emigration from Scotland took place after Cromwell's settlement of Ireland in 1652. It was stated in Parliament, in 1656, (with some exaggeration perhaps), that the Scots in Ireland could "raise 40,000 fighting men." See Harrison, p. 84.

70. Reid, ii. 43, 44.

71. Reid, ii. 344-53, 382, 424; Killen, ii. 136-38; Hamilton, 74-77.

72. This took place in 1670. See the *True Narrative* (*sub fin.*) of Adair, who relates that during the performance the upper gallery fell down, and "divers were killed and many hurt." Reid, ii. 409.

73. Archb. Synge. See Lecky's *England*, ii. 400, 401.

74. Killen, ii. 233, 435, 436.

75. Hamilton, pp. 124-28. "On a platform erected in the open air (at Ballyrashane, near Coleraine) the Rev. Robert Higinbotham, minister at Coleraine, and Mr. John Swanston, probationer of the Secession, hammered at each other during the length of the summer day, in the presence of a prodigious assembly of people." When the Scottish Secession was rent in 1747 into the Burgher and anti-Burgher Synods, the Irish Seceders took sides also; and thus "almost at the very inception of its history, Secederism began to present a divided front" in Ireland. The reunion of Irish Presbyterians took place in 1840, when 292 congregations belonging to the main body united with 141 belonging to the Secession.

76. Killen, ii. 435-42; Hamilton, pp. 146-57.

77. Hamilton, p. 169.

78. According to the census of 1891, out of a population in Ulster of 1,617,877, there were 744,353 Catholics, 427,810 Presbyterians, 361,917 Protestant

Episcopalians, 40,525 Methodists, and 41,885 of other denominations.

LECTURE IV

1. See Moncrieff's "Ancient Alliance between the French and Scots" in *Miscellanea Scotica*, iv. 17-19; Burton's *Scot Abroad*, chaps. i. iv. vi.; Michel's *Les Ecossais en France*, i. 6-8, 11, 12. Michel adduces evidence that in Paris alone, at the close of the thirteenth century, there were nearly sixty tax-paying persons who bore the name Escoz, l'Escot, or some other appellation similarly suggestive of Scottish origin, as their proper surname. A district of the town of Danzig is still called Schottland, in memory of a colony of Scottish weavers who settled there in the fifteenth century. See article on "Scots in France" in *Edinburgh Review*, July 1863.

2. Michel's *Ecoss. en France*, i. 115, 116. This expedition was arranged about the year 1420, in response to an embassy sent by Charles VI. Shortly after, a fresh reinforcement of 5000 men arrived under the Earl of Douglas. See *Miscell. Scot.* iv. 13.

3. Michel, i. 119, 147-49; *Miscell. Scot.* iv. 14, 15, 20, 21; Burton's *Scot Abroad*, i. 37, 40, 41, 48-55. The Scots Guard was established by Charles VII. during his struggle with England, and consisted originally of 200 men who guarded the royal person. The number was afterwards increased to 300. The historical details in *Quentin Durward* are taken from the Memoirs of Philip de Comines. The Guard was nominally retained down to the Revolution of 1789, but Scots had gradually disappeared from it.

4. *Miscell. Scot.* iv. 19.

5. Michel, i. 56; Mackenzie's *Lives of Eminent*

Scottish Writers, ii. 6; article in *Edin. Rev.* Jan. 1864, cxix. 200-202; W. Stephen's *Scottish Church*, i. 413; ii. 558, 559, 610, 611. The Scots College was broken up at the Revolution of 1789. The French Government, about forty years ago, undertook, as compensation for the loss of the old College buildings, "the expense of educating eighteen Scottish students in French seminaries; an arrangement which holds good to the present time."

6. Major's *Hist. of Greater Britain*, B. iii. 11; Dempster, *Hist. Eccl. Gent. Scot.* pp. 567-71; Mackenzie's *Lives*, i. 147-55; Migne's *Patrologia*, cxcvi. pp. ix.-xvi. Richard was a most voluminous writer on exegetical, doctrinal, and practical religious subjects. Among his more notable works are *De Verbo Incarnato, De Trinitate*, and *De Gratia Contemplationis*, the intuition or immediate vision of the divine, as distinguished from "cogitatio" or reasoning. Major describes him as "second to none of the theologians of his generation," and the high esteem in which his writings were held on the Continent in the Middle Ages may be judged from the fact that in 1518 thirty-seven were extant and were published at Paris. They were republished there in 1540, and afterwards in Venice, Cologne, and Rouen. Guilielmus of St. Victor, writing in 1348, when the relations between France and Scotland had become intimate, describes Richard as "Scotus" (Migne). The inscription (1531) on his tomb in the cloister of St. Victor contains the following testimonies to his nationality and to his fame :—

"Quem tellus genuit felici Scotica partu. . . . .
Plurima namque tui superant monumenta laboris,
Quae tibi perpetuum sint paritura decus."

7. Major (1470-1550) speaks of Duns Scotus as a "Scottish Briton born at Duns, a village eight miles distant from England, and separated from my own home (North Berwick) by only seven or eight leagues." The editor, in the fourteenth century, of the Commentary (ascribed to Duns) on Aristotle's *Metaphysics*, speaks of him as "Natione Scotus," and by that time the designation "Scot" meant a native of Scotland, unless there was express indication to the contrary. Rabelais (1483-1553) refers to Duns as "Maistre Jehan d'Ecosse." In 1513 a monument was erected to his memory in a church at Cologne bearing the inscription: "Scotia me genuit: Anglia me suscepit: Gallia me docuit: Colonia me tenet." Antony Possevin (1534-1611) describes Duns as "natus in ulteriore Britannia ad Calydoniam sylvam" (*App. Sac.* i. 868). These testimonies outweigh the following evidence adduced in favour of Down in Ireland and Dunstane in Northumberland. In 1487, O'Fihely, Archishop of Tuam, in a preface to his edition of the Commentary on Aristotle's *Metaphysics*, claims Duns as an Irishman, but gives no definite indication as to his birthplace; and the earliest mention of Down in this connection is by Hugh, Archbishop of Armagh, about the end of the sixteenth century, who writes of Duns as "probably" born there. For the English claim the chief testimony is that of John Leland (1506-52), who, in his *De Scriptoribus Britannicis*, states that in a MS. of Merton College, Oxford, Duns is stated to have been born at Dunstane in Northumberland, but the MS. is not extant, and there is no means of judging whether the statement was more than a mere conjecture. Thomas of Eccleston, writing in the fourteenth century, while expressly distinguishing Hibernia from Scotia, indicates

(*Monumenta Franciscana*) that all Britain north of York was reckoned in the province of Scotia, but the statement is not corroborated. See Major's *Hist.* iv. 16; Dempster's *Hist. Eccl. Gent. Scot.* i. 227-32; Burton's *Scot Abroad*, ii. 13; article by J. M. Rigg in *Dict. Nat. Biog.*

8. Burton aptly remarks (*Scot Abroad*, ii. 16): "Could it be maintained that no one opinion promulgated by Duns Scotus is now believed, yet his thoughts are the stages by which we have reached our present position. He who ruled one-half of the intellectual world for centuries, necessarily gave their shape and consistency not only to the views of those who implicitly followed him, but to those of the later thinkers who superseded him; for there is nothing that more eminently moulds the character of opinions than the nature of those which they supersede."

9. The way had been prepared for belief in the Immaculate Conception of Mary (1) by the over-exaltation of her personality, in particular the appellations of "Theotokos," Mother of God, authorised from the fifth century, and "Queen of Heaven" from the eleventh century); (2) by the simultaneous growth of Mariolatry and multiplication of festivals in the Virgin's honour, including that of her alleged Assumption (from the sixth century); (3) by the doctrine which St. Augustine accepted (although rejected by his leading contemporaries as well as by earlier theologians), and which was prevalent from the sixth century onwards, that Mary was by grace free from actual transgression "propter honorem Domini"; (4) by the doctrine to which Bernard, Buonaventura, Aquinas, and others adhered, that the Virgin was free from original sin, having been purified therefrom prior to birth. The

earliest distinct historical trace of belief in the Immaculate Conception is contained in a letter of St. Bernard (174 in the collection) of date 1140. In this letter he remonstrates with the Canons of Lyons for their unauthorised celebration of a festival in honour of the Virgin's Conception, and for their countenance of the erroneous belief that her conception was immaculate. (A later legend ascribes the origination of this festival to an English Abbot in the eleventh century.) During the twelfth and thirteenth centuries the new doctrine was opposed both by Popes (Innocent II., III., and V.) and by leading Doctors (Peter Lombard, Hugo St. Victor, Albertus Magnus, Buonaventura, Aquinas). The advocacy of Duns Scotus turned the tide of opinion. The story of his triumphant defence of the doctrine at Paris in 1307, against 200 objections of Dominican opponents, is not related till the fifteenth century, and may be a legend; but his support of the doctrine after its supposed decisive overthrow by Aquinas is undoubted (Lib. iii. dis. 3, qu. 1; dis. 18, qu. 1); and the weight of his authority, if not the cogency of his arguments, secured for the dogma the powerful adherence of the Franciscan Order to which he belonged, and the early, if not immediate, endorsement of the University of Paris in which he taught. In 1439 the Reforming Council of Basel, after it had become schismatical according to Romish authority, accepted the doctrine and reprobated the opposite. In 1470 Pope Sixtus IV. imposed mutual toleration on defenders and on opponents of the dogma; and this papal dictum remained in force until the decree of Pius IX. in 1854, although his predecessor Gregory XVI. sanctioned the introduction of the term Immaculate into the service of the Church. See Schaff's *Nicene and Post-Nicene Christianity*, pp. 409-28; Meyrick's articles on "Mary" in Smith's *Bib. Dict.* and *Dict. Christ. Antiquities;* Rigg's article on Duns Scotus in *Dict. Nat. Biog.*; Philip Smith's *Hist. of Church in Middle Ages*, pp. 300-305.

10. *Miscell. Scot.* iv. 16, 18, 19; *Edin. Rev.* for July 1863, vol. cxviii. 237, 249, 250; Michel's *Ecossais en France*, i. 7, 71, 153. Among notable Scots who held important ecclesiastical benefices in France during this period were Robert Ellis, originally a vicar in Caithness, who became Archdeacon at Toulouse in the latter part of the twelfth century, and took a leading part in suppressing heresy there; John Carmichael, who was a military chaplain at the battle of Verneuil in 1425, and, under the name St. Michel, became Bishop of Orleans; Andrew Foreman, afterwards Primate of Scotland, who, early in the sixteenth century, was appointed to the Archbishopric of Bourges; and David (afterwards Cardinal) Beaton, who in 1557 became Bishop of Mirepoix.

11. See article on "Scottish Religious Houses Abroad" in *Edin. Rev.*, Jan. 1864; Wattenbach's *Schotten Klöster in Deutschland*, translated by Dr. Reeves in *Ulster Journal of Archæology*, vol. vii. pp. 227-47, and 295-313; MSS. of James Dennistoun of Dennistoun (including Notes made at Ratisbon in 1836), in Advocates' Library, Edinburgh. The Erfurt Monastery is believed to have been established in 1036 as an offshoot from the more ancient Scoto-Irish monastery at Cologne. That of Ratisbon was founded by Marianus Scotus about the time of the Norman Conquest; but the original buildings were superseded by others in the latter part of the following century, when the existing Romanesque

Church was erected. The Nuremberg Benedictine buildings dated from 1111, and were probably erected on the site of an older Irish foundation. This was certainly the case at Würzburg, where Kilian the Irish-Scot laboured in the seventh century, and where in 1136 the Bishop of that see founded a Scottish monastery in memory of his Celtic predecessor. The Scottish Religious House of Vienna was established by Henry the Lion in 1164, "pro Scotis monachis exulibus." It was first occupied by a colony of monks from Ratisbon. Other Scottish monasteries known to have come into existence at this period were those of Constance (1142) Memmingen, near Ulm (1180), Eichstadt in Bavaria (1194), Kellheim, near Ratisbon (1260), and Oels, near Breslau.

12. John Major, who was born near North Berwick in 1469-70, entered the College of St. Barbe at Paris in 1493, and graduated there as Master in 1496, under the rectorship of a countryman of his own, John Harvey. He then became a Regent, and Teacher of Philosophy in Montaigu College. In 1505 he graduated as Doctor of Divinity, and thereafter lectured on theology in the Sorbonne. His Commentaries on Peter Lombard's *Sentences* (the favourite theological text-book of the age) were published in 1509-17, and parts of the work passed within a few years through five editions. The *History of Greater Britain* was issued in 1521. In the following year Major was induced to repair to Scotland, and became Professor of Theology in Glasgow, where he had John Knox as a pupil. In 1523 he was transferred to St. Andrews, where George Buchanan was among his students. He returned to Paris in 1525, and remained there till 1531. His chief work during this period was the composition of

his *Commentary* on and *Harmony of the Gospels*. The last nineteen years of his life (1531-50) were passed in the University of St. Andrews. In 1547 he was present when John Knox preached there his first sermon in public; and he made no open protest against the Reformer's doctrine.

In philosophy Major was a "Terminist," occupying an intermediate position between Nominalism and Realism, although in the main an adherent of the former system. His aim was to reconcile the prevalent nominalism of his time with the traditional theology. He defended Transubstantiation ("whosoever denies it is a foolish heretic"), as well as saint-worship, image-veneration, compulsory clerical celibacy, and other Romish tenets. In a Dedication of his *Commentary on Matthew* to James Beaton, he commends that prelate for having "manfully removed" (*viriliter sustulisti*) an unhappy follower of the "Lutheran heresy," referring to the martyrdom of Patrick Hamilton. None the less, in the spirit of the Council of Constance, Major was a pronounced Church Reformer. He speaks of "papal excommunication" and "ecclesiastical censures" as penalties which one who is in the right "has no reason to fear." Referring to pluralities and other abuses of ecclesiastical patronage, "those deceive themselves," he writes, "who think that the approval even of the Supreme Pontiff can reconcile such things to the dictates of conscience" (*Com. on Matt.* f. 80). He is equally emphatic in his demand for drastic monastic reform, and in his denunciation of clerical corruption. In 1534 he took the part of a friar (William Airth) who had been condemned as a heretic by Bishop Hepburn of Brechin for preaching against the abuse of so-called miracles and against the licentiousness of the clergy.

In a notable epigram, George Buchanan ridicules Major's works as "abounding in trifles"; and, after quoting his former teacher's own self-depreciatory description of himself as "solo cognomine Major," adds sarcastically, "Nec semper mendax fingere Creta solet." But Buchanan received from Major more probably than he was conscious of acquiring; not only intellectual stimulus but, in particular, those constitutional views of government which were afterwards unfolded in the famous *De jure Regni* (see Lecture VI. note 27). Other notable pupils testified more gratefully to Major's worth and influence. Senalis of Paris, in an Oration (1510) speaks of him as "that incomparable Master, whom I cannot praise as much as he deserves." Louis Coronel of Segovia, one of the editors of Ximenes's famous Bible, writes of him as "our Master" whose "learning will commend him not only to posterity but to eternity."

See *Life of Major* by Dr. Æneas J. G. Mackay, prefixed to A. Constable's Translation of Major's *Greater Britain*, especially pp. xxix. xxxviii. lii. lix.-lxii. lxv. lxxi.-lxxiii. lxxx.-lxxxiii. xciv. cvi.-cviii. cxiv. cxxii.-cxxix. The reference to Major by Melanchthon (quoted in Mackay's Biography) is contained in his *Defence of Martin Luther against the furious Decree of the Parisian Theologasters*, op. i. p. 398).

13. George Buchanan (born at Killearn in 1506) was a student in Paris from 1520 to 1522. He returned to France in 1526, took his mastership two years later, at the Scots College in Paris, and in 1529 was appointed to a Chair in the College of St. Barbe.

He returned to Scotland about 1535, and was entrusted by James V. with the education of one of his natural sons; but his bold satires against the Franciscans led to his imprisonment at St. Andrews. In 1539 he escaped to France and held for three years a professorship of Latin at Bordeaux, where Montaigne was one of his pupils. Between 1544 and 1547 he was a Regent in the College of Cardinal le Moine at Paris; in the latter year he accepted the invitation to Coimbra. His three Scottish colleagues there were John Rutherford, William Ramsay, and his own brother, Patrick Buchanan. The charges brought against him at Coimbra were (1) writing a satirical poem on the Franciscans; (2) speaking against Transubstantiation; (3) eating flesh in Lent. After his liberation from prison and a short sojourn in England, he returned once more to France, and became a Regent in the College of Boncourt at Paris, where he remained until 1555. The five following years were spent by Buchanan, partly in France and partly in Italy, as domestic tutor in the family of the Comte de Brissac. In 1560 he finally returned to Scotland. His recognised influence in continental circles may be estimated from Cardinal Beaton's eager efforts, through the Archbishop of Bordeaux, to secure his apprehension there, and from the successful endeavours made to protect him from molestation. See Irving's *Lives of Scottish Writers*, i. 67-78, and also his *Memoir of George Buchanan;* Burton's *Scot Abroad*, ii. 24-26.

14. Alesius (born at Edinburgh in 1500) wrote at least twenty-eight treatises on various exegetical, dogmatic, and controversial subjects, including *Commentaries on the Psalms*, the *Gospel of St. John*, and several *Epistles of St. Paul*, a pacificatory *Exhortation to Concord*, and con-

troversial works on *Justification* (against Osiander), the *Lord's Supper*, the *Trinity*, etc.

The controversy with Cochlaeus was occasioned by Alesius's *Epistola contra decretum quorundam Episcoporum in Scotia* (published in 1533 at Leipzig), which indicated the exile's continued interest in his native land. He is described by Beza in his *Icones* as a man "dear to all the learned, eagerly embraced by the evangelical Church of Saxony, and warmly cherished and esteemed by her to the day of his death" (1565). "He belonged," writes Professor Ward, "to that generous if sanguine band of divines, of whom Melanchthon was leader and type, to whom no gulf which conscientious effort was incapable of bridging seemed fixed between Lutheranism and Calvinism, or even between the new learning and the *vetus ecclesia*." See Professor A. Mitchell's Pre-Reformation Scotland in the St. Giles's *Lectures on the Scottish Church*, pp. 107-112; Lorimer's *Precursors of Knox*, pp. 167, 241, and *Scottish Reformation*, pp. 29-32, 112-119; M'Crie's *Life of Knox*, note I; and Ward's article in the *Dict. Nat. Biog.*

15. M'Alpine fled from Scotland in 1534 to England (Lecture III. note 7), and remained there till 1540, when he removed to Germany. He received his doctorate in theology at Wittenberg prior to his departure for Denmark. His eminent learning and service to the Protestant cause are acknowledged by Danish historians. On the occasion of his death in 1557, his remains were followed to the grave by the king. John Jonston of St. Andrews describes him as "Christianismi in Dania Instaurator" (M'Crie's *Life of Knox*, Supplement). He was the author of various works in exegetical and dogmatical theology. A close friendship and moral

resemblance existed between Machabaeus and Alesius.
Jonston represents the latter as uttering the lines—

> Qui mea scripta legit, Machabacum cernat in illis:
> Alterutrum noscis, noscis utrumque simul.

The name M'Bee, sometimes applied to M'Alpine, is merely an error occasioned by re-translation from the Latin designation. See Lorimer's *Precursors of Knox*, pp. 185, 186, and *Scottish Reformation*, p. 120; M'Crie's *Life of Knox*, note I; Laing's *Works of Knox*, i. 529.

16. Bellesheim's *Catholic Church of Scotland*, iii. 35 (Trans.); Rankine in Story's *Church of Scotland*, ii. 410; W. Stephen's *Scottish Church*, ii. 32.

17. See article on "Scottish Religious Houses" in *Edin. Rev.*, Jan. 1864, and other authorities mentioned in note 11; also Bellesheim, iii. 247. After the Reformation Scottish Colleges, for the education of the Roman Catholic youth of Scotland and for the training of Scottish priests, were established at Douay (1578), at Rome (1600), and at Madrid (1617), in addition to the old Scots College at Paris (see p. 39). These later institutions, however, had a purely Scottish sphere and scope, and exercised no considerable influence in the countries where they were respectively located.

18. See M'Crie's *Life of Melville*, chap. x. Andrew Duncan, John Sharp, John Welsh, John Forbes, and Robert Durie were all imprisoned (1605), and afterwards banished (1606), for holding an Assembly at Aberdeen without the king's authority (*ibid.* chap. viii.). Duncan had been a Regent at St. Andrews, and subsequently minister of Crail. He was eventually allowed to return to Scotland; but suffered a second imprisonment for nonconformity to the Articles of

Perth (Wodrow's *Life of Duncan*, pp. 4-11). Sharp had been minister of Kilmany in Fife. Welsh had occupied the charge of Ayr. In 1622, after fourteen years of ministry in France, he lost his health and repaired to London, but was not allowed to return to Scotland. When the town of St. Jean d'Angély was besieged by Louis XIII., during his conflict with the Huguenots, and at length capitulated, Welsh continued to preach as usual. The Duc d'Espernon was sent to arrest him, but returned with the answer, "Never man spoke like this man." The preacher, however, when summoned, entered the royal presence, and so impressed the king at once with his spiritual earnestness and with his acceptable views regarding royal independence of ecclesiastical control in the secular sphere, that Louis said at length, "Eh bien, vous seriez mon ministre." On a later occasion when the town was again taken, special orders were given to protect Welsh and to transport him in safety, along with his family, to Rochelle (see Kirkton's *Life of Welsh*, pp. 5, 39-41). John Forbes had been minister of Alford in Aberdeenshire, and was Moderator of the "unauthorised" Assembly at Aberdeen in 1605. He was in 1611 the founder of the Scotch Church at Middelburg, from which he was transferred to Delft in 1621. He died in 1634 (Stephen's *Scottish Church at Rotterdam*, pp. 294, 316). Robert Durie had been minister of Anstruther, and held the Scotch charge at Leyden from 1609 until his death in 1616. He was a frequent correspondent of his nephew Andrew Melville, who addresses him as "Right Reverend and dearly beloved father in the Lord Jesus" (Stephen, p. 312, and M'Crie's *Life of Melville*, Appendix x.).

19. The authorities of La Rochelle applied in 1608

for Melville's liberation, with a view to his appointment to the professorship of Biblical Theology there. The application was without effect; but in 1610 the influential appeal of the Duke of Bouillon, head of the French Protestant party, was successful, and led to Melville being allowed to go to Sedan. Principal Donaldson was a native of Aberdeen, and held the professorship of Natural and Moral Philosophy. Two other Scots were contemporary with Melville at Sedan— John Smith, who occupied a Chair of Philosophy, and John Colville, Professor (successively) of Hebrew and of Theology. Tilenus, originally Melville's colleague in divinity, while professing Calvinism really propagated Arminianism. Melville exposed his duplicity, and was the means of Tilenus leaving Sedan. See James Melville's *Diary*, p. 35; Irving's *Lives of Scottish Writers*, i. 303-306, and M'Crie's *Life of Melville*, chaps. i. ix. and x. Spottiswood's reference to Melville's life and work at Sedan (*Hist.* Book vii., under the year 1606), "He was sent to Sedan, where he lived in no great respect, and lay almost bedfast till his death," is due, doubtless, to prejudiced and unfounded reports which had reached him, and were too readily believed.

20. Cameron (born in 1579) came in 1600 to Bordeaux, where one of the Reformed pastors was a Scot, Gilbert Primrose. His conspicuous attainments in Greek and Latin led in the same year to his appointment as classical professor in the newly-founded College of Bergerac, whence he was transferred in 1601 to a Chair of Philosophy at Sedan. The four years from 1604 to 1608 he spent at Paris, Geneva, and Heidelberg, prosecuting theological study, at the expense of the French Protestant Church, which in this way

showed its high appreciation of his potential services. In 1608 he was appointed to the pastorate in Bordeaux, from which he was translated in 1618 to the Chair of Theology at Saumur. Political troubles in France led to his departure in 1620, and, after about two years' residence in England, he was appointed by James VI. (with whose political ideas and ecclesiastical policy he was in accord) to the Principalship of Glasgow University. Finding himself, however, out of harmony with his colleagues on Church questions, he soon resigned his office and returned to Saumur in 1623. It was found impracticable to reinstate him in his professorship there; but he received a thousand livres from the Huguenot Synod as compensation, and was ere long appointed to the Chair of Divinity at Montauban, where he died in 1625. His death was hastened by an outrage committed upon him by an impetuous Protestant whose indignation had been roused by Cameron's doctrine of passive obedience. See *Life of Cameron* by his pupil Cappel prefixed to the Geneva edition of his works; Irving's *Lives*, i. 333-446; Burton's *Scot Abroad*, ii. 104; Bayle's *Dictionary*; and T. F. Henderson's article in *Dict. Nat. Biog.* Milton, in his "Tetrachordon," refers to Cameron as "an ingenious writer in high esteem."

21. John Forbes of Corse was the son of Bishop Patrick Forbes of Aberdeen, and nephew of John Forbes of Alford (see note 18). He was admitted to the Chair of Theology in Aberdeen University in 1619, at the age of twenty-six. The leaders of the Covenant, who respected him highly, used every influence to win him to their side, but in vain. The *Instructiones* was much lauded by the Theological Faculties of Leyden,

Utrecht, and Franeker, as well as by Vossius, Rivet, and other eminent continental scholars. Forbes returned to Scotland in 1646, and died in 1648. The use of his work (in the abridged form) as a theological text-book in Denmark, about the year 1829, has been certified to me from personal knowledge by his distinguished and venerable namesake, Dr. John Forbes, Professor Emeritus of Hebrew in the University of Aberdeen. Bishop Burnet describes the *Instructiones* as a work which "if he (Forbes) had finished it . . . had been the greatest treasure of theological learning that perhaps the world has yet received." See Garden's *Vita* in the 1702 edition of Forbes's works published at Amsterdam; Irving's *Lives*, ii. 43-54; Rait's *Universities of Aberdeen*, pp. 144-46.

22. Durie was born at Edinburgh in 1596, and was educated for the ministry chiefly at Leyden, where his father was Scottish pastor, and at Sedan under his cousin, Andrew Melville. His earliest attempt at ecclesiastical pacification was in 1628 at Elbing (east of Danzig), where he acted as minister to a congrega- of British merchants. The town was at that time in the hands of Gustavus Adolphus, who cordially supported Durie's project. In addition to the divines mentioned in the text, Durie had the sympathy of Bishops Hall of Exeter, Davenant of Salisbury, and Bedell of Kilmore, as well as of the notable Puritan divine John White of Dorchester. Even Laud, while Bishop of London, gave him some support. Among congresses and conferences at which his views were received with favour may be enumerated those held at Leipzig, Danzig, Hanau, Frankfort, Aargau, and Zurich. Durie's aims and methods are set forth in

forty-eight larger or smaller publications, including his *Summary Discourse on Peace Ecclesiastical* (1641), his *Summary Platform of Practical Divinity* (1654), and his *Irenicorum Tractatuum Prodromus* (1662). In his latest book, *Manière d'expliquer l'Apocalypse* (1674), he unfolds his wider scheme of universal union. "What causes division and hatred among Christians is nothing else but men's resolution to maintain the principles and methods of their particular faction against what the common edification requires. My design, therefore, is to inquire after the truly evangelical and spiritual remedy which may be applied to the consciences of those who, for worldly views, keep up a spirit of faction among Christians. This is the foundation and purpose of my new scheme" (p. 17). See articles in Bayle's *Dictionary*, and in *Dict. Nat. Biog.* (Gibson); Briggs's article in *Pres. Rev.* April 1887.

23. See Lecture III. note 51, and the reference there.

24. See *Memoirs of R. and J. A. Haldane*, by Alexander Haldane, pp. 415, 438, 447, 453-55, 461-66, 470-72.

"During the time of your uncle's sojourn," wrote Professor Gaussen to the biographer of Robert Haldane, "almost all the students in theology attended his expositions. Among them all only one did not appear to be touched; the majority have become eminent in the service of God. The evangelical work of Geneva was the child of Haldane; the work of grace in Vaud was the daughter of that in Geneva; the work in France was to a great extent the child of that of Geneva and Vaud."

At the meeting of the Evangelical Alliance in London

(1851) Merle d'Aubigné declared that "if it had not been for the grace of God in ordering the mission of the venerable Robert Haldane from Scotland, I would not, so far as man can see, have been here to-day." In 1842, when Haldane was on his deathbed, one of the pastors (Marzials) at Montauban wrote to his nephew from personal remembrance, "When he (Haldane) first appeared in our town, the Gospel of salvation was in little honour, and its vital doctrines entirely unknown except by a very few. But, thanks be to God, now in this Church, as in a great many others in France, the truth of God is preached with power . . . the fruit of the good seed sown here and elsewhere by your venerable uncle." The Continental Society, founded in 1818, employed itinerating French and Swiss missionaries.

25. About sixteen years ago, through the efforts of the late Dr. William Robertson of New Greyfriars', Edinburgh, and others, £12,000 were raised for the endowment of the Waldensian ministry. In 1895 Scotland contributed, mainly in the form of annual subscriptions, about £3700 to the Waldensian Missions, and £337 to the Italian Evangelistic Society; over £2000 to the M'All Mission, and nearly £500 to the Evangelisation Society, in France; £1280 to the Evangelical Society of Geneva, and £880 to that of Belgium.

26. See *Report of First General Presbyterian Council*, pp. 25, 26, 242, 245-49, 278, 300. Among the speakers at the Council meetings was Dr. De Pressensé of Paris, who said, "It is a great encouragement to see here unfurled the flag of evangelical liberty, whilst we are obliged in France to carry it in an obscure way. We look to you, and to the great victory which was won at the Reformation in this country, and which

cheers us all. . . . Religion on the Continent will be lost if we cannot show Churches where evangelical truth and unity are joined with liberty. I rejoice to see this great Presbyterian Church which unites in so beautiful and wonderful a way liberty and Gospel truth and a great Christian confederacy." The representative of the Free Evangelical Church of Germany testified that his Church "owed her origin to the Jewish Mission of the Free Church of Scotland." Among letters sent to the Council by distinguished continental Churchmen was one from Dr. Herzog, editor of the *Real Encyclopaedie*, in which he speaks of Scotland as "from the day of John Knox a metropolis of reformed faith and life,"—the country "to which in our century so many men belonging to different Churches have been accustomed to direct their gaze as to an inspiriting example."

LECTURE V

1. Ogilvie's *Presbyterian Churches*, pp. 181-83.
2. *Ibid.* pp. 168-76 ; R. Hamilton's *Jubilee History of the Presbyterian Church in Victoria;* Campbell's *Fifty Years of Presbyterianism in Victoria; Report of Fifth Presbyterian General Council.* Mr. Lang brought five other ministers from Scotland in 1826, to form the original Presbytery. Eventually, in 1842, he seceded from the Church which he had founded, and for which he had been the means of securing State support. He organised a new denomination on voluntary principles. The dependence of the Australian Presbyterians for a ministry on the Churches at home led to further schism

after the Disruption of 1843; but the three sections of Presbyterianism in New South Wales were ultimately re-united in 1865. The Presbyterian Church of Victoria originated in a congregation formed at Melbourne in 1837 by the Rev. James Clow, a retired Indian chaplain of the Church of Scotland. The first Presbytery (of Melbourne) was erected in 1842. The three separate Presbyterian organisations which came into existence (connected with the Church of Scotland, the Free Church, and the U.P. Church respectively) were united in 1859, when the First General Assembly of the Victoria Church was held under the appropriate moderatorship of the venerable founder. The Presbyterian Churches of the other four Australian colonies (West Australia, South Australia, Queensland, and Tasmania) are much smaller, but are increasing in numbers and strength. The total Presbyterian population in Australia is estimated at 300,000.

3. Ogilvie, pp. 176-80; Stuart Ross's *Otago Church;* *Report of Fifth Presbyterian General Council.*

4. *Ibid.*

5. The total number of communicants in the Presbyterian Churches of North America, as reported to the General Presbyterian Council at Glasgow in 1896, was 2,170,000, of whom about 300,000 were of German or Dutch descent. In Canada the number of Presbyterian adherents (including children) is $4\frac{1}{2}$ times that of the communicants. Assuming that the same proportion subsists in the United States, the Presbyterians in North America may be estimated at $9\frac{3}{4}$ millions. In 1894 the Roman Catholic communicants in the United States and Canada together were nearly 10 millions; Methodist communicants about 8 millions;

Baptist, 4¼th millions; Presbyterian, nearly 2 millions; Anglican Episcopalians, ¾ths of a million; Congregationalist, over ⅔rds of a million. The proportion of communicants to adherents is very much larger in the Roman Catholic Church than in Protestant Churches. See Ogilvie, p. 196; Carroll's *Religious Forces in the United States*, pp. xxxv. 457.

6. Archbishop Laud contemplated the appointment of a Bishop of New England, but he was diverted from his purpose, probably by home distractions. After the Restoration, Clarendon proposed four colonial bishoprics; but the scheme was frustrated by his political fall. Later still, Queen Anne, at the instigation of the English hierarchy, resolved to found an American episcopate; but she died before her resolution could be carried into effect. See *Church Quarterly Review*, xix. 439.

7. Skinner's *Annals of Scottish Episcopacy*, pp. 58-64; Walker's *Life of Skinner*, pp. 38-46; Skinner Wilson's *Seabury Centenary; Church Quarterly Review*, xix. 427-47. Three years after Seabury's consecration, two other bishops, Drs. White and Prevoost (the former elected by the episcopal clergy of Philadelphia, the latter by those of New York), were consecrated at Lambeth by the Primate and three other prelates. A regular succession was thus secured for the American episcopate without further British intervention. The character and tone of early American episcopacy was largely due to Scottish episcopal influences. Many of the Scottish episcopal clergy, ejected after 1690, had emigrated to America; by the concordat between Seabury and the Scottish bishops, the former pledged himself to labour for a substantial agreement between the two Churches, especially regarding the celebration of the Eucharist;

and to this day the American Episcopal Church uses a modification of the Scottish Communion office.

8. Briggs's *American Presbyterianism*, p. 90. Stirke was there from 1623 to 1636. Copland came in 1633.

9. Samuel Skelton and Francis Higginson, from Lincolnshire and Leicestershire respectively. See Cotton Mather's *Magnalia Christi Americana*, B. i. 4. 4.; Briggs, p. 93.

10. Hodge's *Presbyterian Church in the U.S.* i. 214. "From the middle of the seventeenth to the middle of the eighteenth century, Presbyterians were the most numerous class of emigrants, and probably more numerous than all other classes combined. The Congregationalists who associated with them entered the Church under the name of Presbyterians." Hodge estimates the Presbyterian emigrants before 1750 as between one and two hundred thousand (i. 60).

11. Cotton Mather's *Magnalia*, B. i. 5. 7.

12. See Lecture III. p. 73.

13. R. Webster's *History of the Presbyterian Church in America*, p. 66. A list of the prisoners in one of the ships sent out at this time is preserved in the collections of the Massachusetts Historical Society.

14. Burton's *History of Scotland*, vii. 176, 234, 277 (ed. 1876); Bancroft's *History of the Colonisation of the United States*, ii. 410, 411; Webster, pp. 66, 68; Shields's *Hind let loose*, p. 201. Many of those concerned, or accused of being concerned, in the Pentland Rising (1666) were condemned to transportation and servitude. The same sentence was pronounced upon 250 Covenanters in 1679, after the battle of Bothwell Bridge, and also upon 100 of the Dunnottar captives in 1685; but in the former case shipwreck substituted death for

NOTES

nd to ···   American Episcopal Church uses
odifica···   Scottish Communion office.
  8. Br··   ···, *Presbyterianism*, p. 90. Stir
was then ·   ··; to 1636. Copland came in 163
  9. S···   ton and Francis Higginson, fro
incoln·l·   Leicestershire respectively. S
otton M   ···*et Christi Americana*, B. i. 4. 4
riggs, p
 10. H·   *··rian Church in the U.S.* i. 21
"From ·l·   · of the seventeenth to the middle
the eigh·   ·ury, Presbyterians were the mo
numerou·   emigrants, and probably mo
numerou·-   other classes combined. The Co
gregation ·   associated with them entered t
Church "·   name of Presbyterians." Hod
estimate   ·yterian emigrants before 1750
between ···   · o hundred thousand (i. 60).
 11. C·   · her's *Magnalia*, B. i. 5. 7.
 12. S··   III. p. 73.
 13. R·   *History of the Presbyterian Church*
America, p   list of the prisoners in one of t
ships sent ··· ·s time is preserved in the collectio
of the M -   Historical Society.
 14. Bu·   *·tory of Scotland*, vii. 176, 234, 2
(ed. 1876·   ·t's *History of the Colonisation of* ·
United St··   111; Webster, pp. 66, 68; Shield
Hind let ··· 01. Many of those concerned,
accused ·t · · oncerned, in the Pentland Risi
(1666) wer   ·ned to transportation and servitu·
The same ··· ···as pronounced upon 250 Covena
ters in 167·· · he battle of Both···· Bridge, a·
also upon l· · ·· Dunnottar c····· ····685; l·
in the form·· · shipwreck

bondage, while in the latter the majority died of fever on the voyage, and the remainder, on their arrival in New Jersey, were declared by the colonial magistrates to be free men (Cunningham's *History of the Church of Scotland*, ii. 121, 139).

15. See the "Brief Advertisement concerning East New Jersey in America," appended to George Scot of Pitlochie's *Model of the Government of the Province of East New Jersey, and encouragements for such as design to be concerned there* (Edin. 1685). The book contains a collection of letters from colonists to their friends at home.

16. See Hodge, i. 57; Webster, p. 68; Briggs, pp. 114, 119, 120, App. lii. Dr. Hodge, on the authority of an MS. by Dr. Balch of Georgetown, endorses the tradition that the pastor, Nathaniel Taylor, came from Fife with the colonists; Briggs regards it as more probable that he was imported from New England. Taylor was one of the seven who constituted the first Presbytery in America (see note 30).

17. Hodge, i. 58; Bancroft, ii. 173. Lord Cardross himself returned to Scotland after the Revolution (Malcolm Laing's *History of Scotland*, iv. p. 187). Ramsay (*History of South Carolina*, ii. 23, quoted by Hodge) states that "to the Scotch South Carolina is indebted for much of its early literature. A great proportion of its physicians, clergymen, lawyers, and schoolmasters were from North Britain."

18. Webster, pp. 69-71; Briggs, p. 122. The leader of the enterprise (1685) was George Scot of Pitlochie (see note 15), who died on the voyage. Riddel had been minister of Kippen prior to his imprisonment from 1677 to 1685. He returned thither

after the Revolution. Frazer also returned and became minister of Alness.

19. George Scot of Pitlochie's *Province of East New Jersey*, p. 268.

20. Bancroft, ii. 410. "This is the era at which East New Jersey, till now chiefly colonised from New England, became the asylum of Scottish Presbyterians." In 1684, twenty-two emigrants sailed from Glasgow under William Dunlop (afterwards Principal of Glasgow University) as pastor, and settled at Port Royal on Broad River (Briggs, p. 127). In 1685 there is the record of a Presbyterian congregation at Brookhaven under the pastorate of Dugald Simpson, who had been a student at Glasgow (*ibid.* p. 106).

21. Smith's *History of New York*, p. 177 (quoted by Hodge, i. 56).

22. Bancroft, ii. 412. The words quoted were written in 1837.

23. See Briggs, p. 128. "The majority of the ministers and people sought refuge in New England." Stobo settled in South Carolina, became pastor of the Puritan congregation at Charlestown, and devoted his life to the establishment of Presbyterianism in that colony.

24. Holme's *American Annals*, ii. 131, 142, 145; Williamson's *History of North Carolina*, ii. 80; and Ramsay's *History of South Carolina*, ii. 16, 25 (quoted by Hodge, i. 55-59, 72, 73); Bancroft, iii. 427. Holmes mentions the arrival of 400-500 emigrants from Scotland at New York in 1737; Williamson speaks of 500-600 Scotsmen settling in North Carolina in 1749, of a second immigration in 1754, and of an "annual importation of these hardy and industrious people" into the province. Ramsay testifies to Scotch settle-

ments in South Carolina during the same period. Similar testimony is given by Hodge to settlements in Pennsylvania and Virginia; and Bancroft refers to early immigration of Scotch Highlanders into Georgia before the middle of the eighteenth century.

25. Briggs, p. 184; Croskery's *Irish Presbyterianism*, p. 13; Hamilton's *Irish Presbyterian Church*, p. 110.

26. Hodge, i. 57, 74; Briggs, pp. 184-191. Hodge refers to a letter, of date 1730, which speaks of "such a multitude of people coming in from Ireland of late years" to Pennsylvania; and Briggs quotes a letter from an Ulster minister in 1718, who refers to the "great desolation" caused there by ministers "demitting their congregations," and by "great numbers of their people going with them."

27. R. Ellis Thompson's *Presbyterian Churches in the United States*, p. 23.

28. Proud's *History of Pennsylvania* (1797-98), ii. 273. Holmes (*American Annals*, ii. 123) estimates the number in 1729 as 6000. The stream of emigration continued in the latter part of the century; for Holmes testifies (ii. 305) that during one fortnight in August 1773 the arrivals in Pennsylvania from Ireland amounted to 3500. See Hodge, i. 57.

29. Ellis Thompson, p. 22.

30. Francis Makemie, Geo. M'Nish, John Hampton, and John Boyd. Of the remaining four, one (Nathaniel Taylor) is regarded by Webster (p. 318) and Hodge (i. p. 57) as a Scot. See note 16.

31. Briggs, p. 280.

32. *Ibid.* p. 290.

33. Hodge, i. 18.

34. *Ibid.* ii. 243, 245. The deputies (Gilbert

Tennent and Samuel Davies) stated that in "the colonies of New York, New Jersey, Pennsylvania, Maryland, Virginia, and Carolina, a great number of congregations have been formed on the Presbyterian plan," and have "put themselves under the synodical care of your petitioners, who conform to the constitution of the Church of Scotland, and have adopted her standard of doctrine, worship, and discipline." "If I am prejudiced," wrote Davies, "in favour of any Church, my Lord, it is of that established in Scotland; of which I am a member in the same sense that the established Church in Virginia is the Church of England."

35. Hodge, ii. 308, 309; Webster, p. 623; Briggs, p. 321. The minister referred to was Samuel Harker, who held Arminian views of grace. He is believed to have been of Huguenot descent.

36. Briggs, p. 328.

37. *Ibid.* p. cxix. The writer quotes the letter (embodying the resolution) addressed to the General Assembly of 1770.

38. *Ibid.* pp. 175, 176. He quotes the minutes of the Synod of Glasgow on the subject.

39. *Ibid.* p. 182.

40. The collection in 1752 was for the supply of ordinances to Swiss and German emigrants in Pennsylvania; another in 1754 was for the New Jersey Presbyterian College; the third in 1760 was for the relief of poor Presbyterian ministers and of ministers' widows and children. See Briggs, pp. 322, civ. cxi. cxii. cxvii.; Webster, p. 260.

41. Briggs, pp. 300-302.

42. Webster, p. 604; Briggs, pp. 324, 325, who quotes from Sprague's *Annals*, iii. 191-94. Occom was

an Indian of the Mohegan tribe, and was ordained by the Presbytery of Suffolk in 1759. He was the "first Indian preacher who had appeared in Great Britain."

43. In 1713, the Presbytery of Glasgow sent out Robert Witherspoon to Pennsylvania, giving him £40 to "fit him out" (Briggs, p. 109). In 1732, the same Presbytery despatched Alexander Hutcheson to Maryland, and "paid his expenses to America" (Briggs, p. 193). In 1725, John Deane and William Maxwell were selected by the Synod of Glasgow for pastorates in South Carolina (Briggs, p. 223). In 1735, the Presbytery of Edinburgh, under the auspices of the Society for Promoting Christian Knowledge, ordained John MacLeod of Skye for ministry to a Highland colony in Georgia (Briggs, p. 329). In 1751 the Reformed Presbyterian Church sent out John Cuthbertson to Pennsylvania (Ellis Thompson, p. 41). In 1753-54 the Anti-Burgher Synod commissioned Alexander Gellatly, Andred Arnot, and James Proudfoot to organise a Presbytery in the same colony. In 1768, the Burgher Synod sent out Messrs. Edmond and and Mitchell (Briggs, p. 340).

44. Briggs, pp. 163, 171, 175, 181, 192, lxxiii. lxxxiii. lxxxvii.

45. Webster's Biographies, appended to his *History*, pp. 297-619; biographical notes in Hodge, i. 80-84, 188-90; Briggs, *passim*.

46. Webster, p. 318; Briggs, pp. 139, 156, etc. M'Nish came to Maryland from London in 1705 with Francis Makemie (see note 49); but he was a Glasgow student, and the entry in connection with his matriculation there indicates that he was a native of Scotland.

47. Webster, pp. 340, 341; Briggs, pp. 208, 246.

Gillespie came from Glasgow to New England in 1712. He published in 1735 a "Treatise against the Deists or Freethinkers, shewing the necessity of Revealed Religion." His contemporary, Francis Alison, describes him as "that pious saint of God."

48. Briggs, pp. 332, 351, and Ellis Thompson, pp. 46, 52, etc.; *Encyclopaedia Americana*, iv. 784; Ogilvie's *Presbyterian Churches*, p. 140. (See also Lecture VI. p. 190.) Witherspoon was minister at Beith and at Paisley, successively, before his removal from Scotland. He wrote *Ecclesiastical Characteristics* against the Moderates in 1753, a treatise on *Justification* in 1756, and another on *Regeneration* in 1764. His collected works were published in Philadelphia and in Edinburgh after his death. He had invitations to occupy important spheres in Dublin and in Rotterdam prior to his appointment in 1706 to the Presidency of Princeton College. The study of Hebrew and of French was introduced by him into the curriculum of that College, and he was the first to deliver lectures to the students. Along with his principalship he held the pastorate of Princeton congregation, and he soon became the recognised leader of the Church, under whom, in 1789, the first General Assembly was held. He received the degree of D.D. from Aberdeen in 1764.

49. Webster, pp. 297-310; Briggs, pp. xliv. etc., 116-18, 139, 140, 152. Ogilvie's *Presbyterian Churches*, p. 135. Makemie (1658-1708) was a native of Ramelton in Ulster, a student of Glasgow University, and a licentiate of the Presbytery of Laggan in Ireland (1681). He emigrated to America in 1683, as pastor of a band of colonists, and for about ten years was an itinerant evangelist, supporting himself by mercantile pursuits.

Between 1693 and 1698 he was pastor of a church in the Barbadoes, after which he settled in Maryland. In 1704 he visited London and returned with two young colleagues, M'Nish and Hampton, alumni, like himself, of Glasgow. His arrest, in 1706, for illegal preaching was by the despotic order of Lord Cornbury, who claimed that the Toleration Act was not sufficient to warrant "dissenters" preaching without a special provincial licence. Makemie's acquittal and the irritation of the Puritans against the Governor led to the latter's recall.

50. Webster, pp. 364-67 ; Briggs, pp. 186, 242, 256, 304 ; Ellis Thompson, p. 30. William Tennent graduated at Edinburgh University in 1695, and was ordained by the Bishop of Down as deacon in 1704, and as priest in 1706 ; but after his arrival in Pennsylvania, in 1710, he became a Presbyterian. Webster declares that to "William Tennent above all others is owing the prosperity and enlargement of the Presbyterian Church" (in America). Whitefield in his Diary calls him "an old gray-headed disciple and soldier of Jesus Christ, blessed with four gracious sons."

51. Webster, pp. 440-43 ; Briggs, pp. 245, 261-63, 267, 304, 305, 326. Alison (1705-79) studied at Glasgow University, and came to America as a probationer in 1734. In 1741 he signed the "Protestation" against the admission into Church Courts of any who had not adopted and subscribed the Westminster standards ; but he was not an extreme adherent of his party, and on the occasion of the re-union in 1758 he preached and published a notable sermon with the title *Peace and Union recommended*. He established at New London, where he was minister, and afterwards at

Philadelphia, an academy which the "Old Side" adopted as its training college.

52. In 1724, the Presbytery of Newcastle (Am.) began to exact subscription to the Westminster Confession, and in 1728 that Presbytery memoralised the Synod to make subscription universal. This memorial constrained the Church officially to face the question.

53. Subscription of the Westminster Confession by ministers had not been enjoined when that Confession was approved by the General Assembly of the Church of Scotland in 1647, but had been introduced after the Revolution, with the immediate object of protecting the Church from the continuance of heretical Episcopalians in her ministry. In the Presbyterian Church of Ireland subscription was introduced in 1698, but was at first required only from licentiates. The obligation was in 1705 extended to ministers at ordination, owing, partly, to the appearance of Arian or semi-Arian heresy. Cunningham's *Church of Scotland*, ii. 174, 181; Hamilton's *Irish Presbyterian Church*, p. 110.

54. Briggs, pp. 216-21; Hodge, pp. 127-30; Webster, pp. 103, etc. Dr. Briggs brings out clearly the influence of the Irish Pacific Act of 1720 in the framing of the American enactment. The Pacific Act had decreed that, "if any person called on to subscribe shall scruple any phrase or phrases in the Confession, he shall have leave to use his own expressions, which the Presbytery shall accept of, providing they judge such a person sound in the faith, and that such expressions are consistent with the substance of the doctrine."

55. Briggs, pp. 250-72.

56. See Cunningham's *Church of Scotland*, ii. 246, 247, 267-74, 302, 303, 322-25; Niven and Milroy in

Story's *Church of Scotland,* iii. 617, 632-38, 667, 679-81, iv. 249-51, 261-65, 279-81; Briggs, pp. 204-206, lxxxviii. In the first Simson case (1717) the General Assembly merely enjoined him not to use certain expressions capable of heterodox meaning; in the second (1726-29) he was held to have denied the necessary existence of the Son of God, and the numerical oneness in substance of the Trinity; but in consideration of alleged retractations, he was not deposed, but only suspended. Campbell was accused (1736) of denying that the Being and attributes of God were discoverable without supernatural instruction, and was admonished to be "cautious, and not to use doubtful expressions." Wishart was accused (1738) of "profanely diminishing the due influence of arguments taken from future rewards and punishments." He was not only acquitted but afterwards raised to the Moderator's Chair. Leechman was charged (1744) with ignoring, in a treatise on prayer, the necessity of Christ's mediation, but was absolved on the ground that he had elsewhere expressed his belief in that truth.

57. M'Kerrow's *History of the Secession,* i. 207, 214; Cunningham's *Church of Scotland,* ii. 314-17.

58. Briggs, pp. 318-21.

59. Hodge's *Presbyterian Law,* pp. 312, 379, 382. "System of faith" is the expression used in the ordination of ministers; "system of doctrine" in that of elders.

60. Presbyterianism, under French auspices, was planted in North America before the close of the sixteenth century, and in the seventeenth century there were numerous communities of Huguenot Presbyterians in Canada; but after the Revocation of the Edict of

Nantes, in 1685, this element of the French-Canadian population was virtually extinguished. See Ogilvie's *Presbyterian Churches*, pp. 153, 154.

61. See Gregg's *History of the Presbyterian Churches in Canada*; Ogilvie, pp. 154-58; Campbell's *History of the Scotch Presbyterian Church, St. Gabriel Street, Montreal*, chaps. ii. and iii.

62. Notable among these was Bishop Strachan of Toronto, who emigrated from Scotland to Canada in the end of the eighteenth century, and took a leading part in the organisation of the Episcopal Church. See Campbell, chap. xii. Strachan had been a student in King's College, Aberdeen, and to the end, his preaching, as well as his character, was of the Scottish type.

63. Carroll's *Religious Forces of the United States*, Introduction, p. xxxv.

64. See statistics in Chambers's *Encyclopædia*, v. 379.

65. See address by Dr. Cochrane of Brentford in *Report of Third General Presbyterian Council*, p. 255-59; and address by Dr. Robertson of Winnipeg in *Report* of the Fifth General Council at Toronto, p. 207.

66. Carroll, pp. xxxvi. 457. The Presbyterian Churches of the United States have about 16½ per cent of the total Protestant population.

67. Carroll, pp. 68, 69.

68. Ellis Thompson, pp. 74, 75. The licensing by the Cumberland Presbytery of some earnest young men who had not received full academic training and had not given an unqualified assent to the Confession of Faith, led in 1810 to a rupture, and to the eventual establishment of the Cumberland Presbyterian Church as a separate denomination.

69. Moberly's Bampton Lectures, p. 68 and App.; Paper by Dr. John Cairns in *Report of First General Presbyterian Council*, p. 56.

70. A President of the United States issued, some years ago, an order enforcing "observance of the Sabbath by officers and men in the military and naval service." The order condemns "profanation of the day," and declares that a due regard for the Divine will, "as well as other considerations, demand that Sunday labour be reduced to the measure of strict necessity." See *Report of First General Presbyterian Council*, p. 222.

71. *Ibid.* pp. 130-33, and 206, where the testimony of a prominent American organ of the R. C. Church is quoted to the services of the Presbyterian Churches: "Their intellectual and moral worth, their philanthropy and zeal for God, the value of many most excellent works which they have written in defence of the Divine Revelation, we fully appreciate. . . . We desire that . . . the Catholic Church in the United States may be strengthened by the accession of that intellectual and religious vigour which such a great mass of baptized Christians contains in itself." The first Temperance Society in America was established by a Presbyterian divine, Albert Barnes. His book, also, on American slavery, was "a thesaurus to the Abolitionists for twenty years." See Ellis Thompson, 130, 132. The names of Edward Robinson, W. M. Thomson, the Hodges, Albert Barnes, Philip Schaff, James M'Cosh, Theodore Cuyler, W. S. Plumer, W. H. Green, W. G. T. Shedd, F. L. Patton, A. T. Pierson, C. A. Briggs, G. M. Grant, are only a few out of many American Presbyterian divines who, in different departments of theological and religious literature, have

exerted a notable influence in America, and also in Great Britain.

72. *Report of First General Presbyterian Council*, pp. 326-28; Ellis Thompson, pp. 197, 198.
73. *Ibid.* pp. 198, 199.

LECTURE VI

1. Adamnan's *Life of St. Columba*, Book iii. chap. vi.
2. See Lecture I. p. 13, and note 27.
3. The general claim of the English Church, as represented by the Archbishop of Canterbury, to jurisdiction over Scotland, rested partly on the shadowy basis of an assignation, by Pope Gregory the Great to St. Augustine, of authority over the bishops of Britain; and partly on the unstable foundation of the treaty of Falaise in 1174. By this treaty William the Lion, under constraint as a prisoner, signed away to Henry II. of England his country's independence, as the price of his own liberation, and the Scottish bishops, with "dexterous diplomacy," agreed to recognise such supremacy of the English over the Scottish Church "as by right it ought to have" (Hailes's *Annals of Scotland*, i. 130, ed. 1797). The treaty, however, was revoked in 1189 by Richard I. for a money consideration (Burton's *Hist. of Scotland*, ii. 3). The special claim of the Archbishop of York rested mainly on the undoubted fact that the portion of Scotland between the Forth and the Solway, prior to its absorption by Scotland in the tenth century, had been under the jurisdiction of his predecessors. When the See of Glasgow was re-

vived in 1114, the Archbishop of York claimed the bishop as a suffragan; the reconstituted diocese including Teviotdale, which had formerly been part of the diocese of Durham (Skene's *Celtic Scotland*, ii. 375). Similarly, the See of Whithorn had been temporarily reconstituted in 731, at a time when Galloway was a province of Northumbria. The Bishop of Whithorn, accordingly, had become a suffragan of York (Bede's *Eccles. History*, v. 23); and when the bishopric was permanently revived under David I., the English assertion of ecclesiastical jurisdiction had been renewed. In 1155, Pope Adrian IV. was induced to homologate the claim of York to authority over the entire Scottish Church, with the exception of the Sees of Orkney and the Isles, which, at that period, were still subject to the Norwegian Metropolitan of Drontheim (Stephen's *Scottish Church*, i. 274, 275).

4. See Fordun's *Annals*, xv. (in *Historians of Scotland*, iv. 262); Burton's *Hist. of Scot.* ii. 3, 4; Cunningham's *Church of Scotland*, i. 102, 103. The presiding legate was Cardinal Petroleonis; there were present King Henry II. of England, William the Lion of Scotland, the Archbishops of Canterbury and York, six Scottish prelates, and other ecclesiastical dignitaries. Henry demanded, and the legate at first advised, the submission of the Scottish clergy; but the cause of Scotland was ably maintained on historical grounds by Gilbert, a canon of Moray, who showed that the Scottish Church had not only been from the first independent of the English, but had taken a leading part in founding the latter; and a dispute between the two archbishops, as to whether the submission claimed by the Church of England was due directly to York or Canterbury, issued in the

Council being closed without a judgment. The way was thus prepared for the Bull of Clement III. in 1188.

5. See Jos. Robertson's *Statuta Eccl. Scot.* Pref. xxxix.; Hailes, i. 144; Cunningham, i. 106. The diocese of Galloway was excepted, and continued to be under the jurisdiction of York until 1358.

6. *Sir William Wallace*, x. 1003-6.

> The Roman buikis that than war in Scotland
> He gart be brocht to scham (shame), where they them fand ;
> And, but radem (redeem), they brynt them thar, ilk ane—
> Salisbury use our clerkis than have tane.

But, in the Moray Chartulary, is a statute of date 1242 appointing Sarum use in that diocese; and the same liturgy was established at Dunkeld before 1249, and in Glasgow by Bishop Herbert, who died in 1164. See Innes in *Spalding Miscellany*, vol. ii. pp. 364-66.

7. "The breaking of an oath . . . like all other offences, has to be measured by the special conditions and prevalent doctrines of the time" (Burton, ii. 258). An oath obtained by coercion is invalid. Under the feudal system, moreover, "every transaction between superior and vassal was made an occasion for oaths"; so that reverence for an oath was undermined; and the Church was believed to have the power of absolution. Burns, *Scot. War of Independence*, ii. 170, 171.

8. Robert Bruce, both the Comyns (Buchan and Badenoch), the Earls of Dunbar and Angus, with others, held English estates, which would be forfeited on their engaging in war with England (Burns, ii. 54-58). Bruce, who was of Norman descent on the paternal side, took an oath of allegiance to Edward during Baliol's reign, and up to the time of Wallace's execution lived much at

the English Court (Burton, ii. 235). After Wallace's victory at Stirling, missives were sent to numerous Scottish nobles, including Angus, Buchan, Badenoch, Dunbar, Lennox, Menteith, Strathearn, and Sutherland, praising them for their fidelity to Edward (Tytler's *History of Scotland*, i. 144, 145). Up till 1301, Simon Frazer, who eventually was executed by Edward I., served under and received favours from that King (Burns, ii. 96, 97). The unpatriotic jealousy entertained towards Wallace by Scottish nobles led to treacherous dealings prior to the battle of Falkirk (Burns, ii. 32). Fordun plainly ascribes the Falkirk defeat to treason among the nobles, especially the Comyns (*Annals*, cii.). After the capture of Stirling by the English in 1304, the leading nobles accepted life, liberty, and estates from Edward on the terms of allegiance to him, although the covenant significantly excluded Wallace, whom Sir John Menteith captured and surrendered. He received a large reward for the service (Fordun's *Annals*, cxvi.; Burton, ii. 224-26; Burns, ii. 130-34). Bruce also suffered from the vacillation and hostility of the nobles (Fordun's *Annals*, cxviii.; Hailes, ii. 1; Burns, ii. 196-205). Even after the death of Edward I., Scottish barons rendered homage to Edward II. (Burns, ii. 259).

9. *Book of Pluscarden*, viii. 11; Wyntoun's *Chronicle*, Book viii. chap. v. 817-44; Hailes, i. 220.

10. Fordun's *Annals*, lxxxvi.; Bower's continuation of Fordun's *Scotichronicon*, xi. 18; Hailes, i. 260. The Abbot barely escaped alive after delivering his message.

11. Grub's *Eccl. Hist. of Scot.* i. 345. The battering-rams were used in the siege of Kirkintilloch, which was in the hands of the English. Wishart had received

the oaks from the English Government in 1291 out of Ettrick forest; but he probably reasoned that as the timber was not really Edward's to give, the gift entailed no obligation to refrain from using it against Edward's representatives. Fordun (*Annals*, xciii.) speaks of the indissoluble bond of love between the elder Robert Bruce (grandfather of the King) and this Bishop of Glasgow.

12. Burton, ii. 202, 237; Burns, ii. 180, 181. In June 1305, before Bruce had openly declared his policy, Lamberton met him at Cambuskenneth; and they signed together a solemn indenture, by which they "engaged that in all their affairs they would give mutual assistance to the utmost of their power."

13. Bellesheim's *Cath. Church of Scot.* (Eng. Trans.), ii. 9-11; Burton, ii. 208; Burns, ii. 88, 93, 94.

14. Burton, ii. 257, 258; Burns, ii. 276-78. The document was signed by the entire episcopate in the name of the "bishops, abbots, priors, and the rest of clergy in the kingdom of Scotland." The translator of Bellesheim mentions (ii. 18, note) the opinion of some that this Council of Dundee was a General Council of the *Estates;* but the document (still preserved among the national MSS.) distinctly shows its clerical origin, and the labels for seals, still remaining, bear the names of bishops.

15. "Loricatos et armatos." See Hailes, ii. 15, 16.

16. Burns, ii. 189. He quotes from an English chronicle of the period.

17. Barbour's *Bruce*, Canto cxx.; Hailes, ii. 83. St. Clair received from Bruce the designation "my own bishop," in recognition of his prowess. He afterwards

sided with the younger Baliol in his usurpation against David II. Hailes, ii. 172.

18. Bower's continuation of Fordun's *Scotichronicon*, xii. 21; *Book of Pluscarden*, ix. 12; Tytler's *History of Scotland*, i. 312 (ed. 1828).

19. Hailes, ii. 4, 15, 20, 103-107; Tytler, i. 229-32, 368-71; Burns, ii. 188-92. "Lamberton's friendship disarmed of its dreadful consequences that sentence of excommunication which was soon thundered against him (Bruce), and his powerful influence interested on his (Bruce's) behalf the whole body of the Scottish clergy" (Tytler, i. 229). Immediately after the slaughter of Comyn, Lamberton, Wishart, David of Moray, and the Abbot of Scone publicly joined Bruce. "Throughout the whole struggle that followed, in spite of repeated Bulls, the native clergy, generally speaking, continued to perform their functions, and thus rendered the papal thunder of comparatively little effect" (Burns, ii. 192).

20. Green's *Short Hist. of the English People*, i. 394-98; Lingard's *Hist. of England*, ii. 455-68 (ed. 1819); Pearson's *England during Early and Middle Ages*, ii. 395-401, 479-85; Burns's *War of Independence*, ii. 458-63; Burton, ii. 232; Russell's *Modern Europe*, i. 407. In 1299 and 1301, after Wallace's victories, Edward made promises not to "raise taxes save by general consent of the realm." To the ancient charters was appended a declaration (1) that "no tallage or aid should henceforth be laid or levied without the goodwill and common consent of the archbishops, bishops, earls, barons, knights, *burgesses*, and *other freemen* of our realm"; (2) that "no officer should take goods of any person without the goodwill and assent of the owner"; (3) that both clergy

and laity of our realm should have their laws, liberties, and free customs as freely and wholly as at any time when they had them best" (Lingard, ii. 465). Edward procured from the Pope in 1305 absolution from these engagements; but "his hand was stayed" by the renewal of the struggle with Scotland under Bruce. In 1309 "it was only by conceding rights of imposing import duties upon the merchants that Edward (II.) procured a subsidy for the Scotch war" (Green).

21. Burton, in *Blackwood's Magazine* for Nov. 1862, p. 547, writes: "The stay and support of France, at that terrible juncture, was chiefly the Scots auxiliaries. With these in his own (the English) ranks, instead of fighting against them, it is easy to see how totally different would have been the strength of the invader." Cf. Burns's *War of Independence*, ii. 465.

22. Macaulay's *Hist. of England*, i. 15: "Had the Plantagenets succeeded in uniting all France under their Government, it is probable that England would never have had an independent existence"; Burns, ii. 466.

23. Stanley's *Life of Thomas Arnold*, ii. p. 406.

24. Major's *Greater Britain*, iv. 17; *In Lib. IV. Lomb. Sent.* f. lxxvi. (Constable's Trans. of *Greater Britain*, p. 158).

25. Laing's *Knox*, ii. 282 (Book iv. of *History*, under 1561).

26. *Defensio Secunda*, p. 137; M'Crie's *Knox*, note MM.

27. Hume Brown's *George Buchanan*, pp. 269, 270. In 1664, also, the Privy Council of Scotland interdicted the translation and circulation of the treatise. In the *De Jure, etc.*, Buchanan lays down the principles (1)

that Acts, after discussion by the representatives of all orders, should be "ultimately referred to the people for sanction"; (2) that if a monarch "extort obedience by force, the people, on the first prospect of superiority in the contest, may shake off so grievous a yoke."

28. Irving's *Memoirs of Geo. Buchanan*, pp. 249-55; Hume Brown, pp. 270, 290, 291; articles in *N. B. Review*, xlviii., and in *Dict. Nat. Biog.* Three editions of the treatise appeared in three successive years. A continental correspondent, to whom Buchanan had sent a copy, describes the eagerness of learned men to have a look of it, and relates how the importunity of friends prevented himself from reading it. The popularity of the work continued in the seventeenth century. During the Civil Wars its notoriety and influence in England are attested by the following epigram:

> A Scot and Jesuit,[1] hand in hand,
> First taught the world to say
> That subjects ought to have command,
> And monarchs to obey.

Even in the eighteenth century three fresh editions were published. Among the many assailants of the work were Ninian Wingate and Blackwood, in the sixteenth century, Sir. Thos. Craig, Sir G. Mackenzie, and (on the Continent) Arnisæus, in the seventeenth. Among those who endorsed Buchanan's views were Milton, Algernon Sidney, and Locke.

29. Burton, vi. 132: Clarendon, *Hist. of Reb.* i. 106, who testifies that "the Book of Canons was thought no other than a subjection to England."

30. Cunningham's *Church of Scotland*, i. 366, 522,

[1] Mariana, author of *De Rege et Regis Institutione*.

525, 529; Burton, vi. 111, 112, 160, 161. In his sermon as Moderator of General Assembly, in 1582, Andrew Melville declaimed against "the bloody gully of absolute authority." "That the innovations, resting on the sole authority of the Crown, without any sanction from the Estates or General Assembly, were an invasion of the constitution and of the national liberties, was the main position held by the supplicants" (Burton).

31. Carlyle's *Inaugural Address to the Students of Edinburgh University*, p. 63; cf. Burns's *War of Independence*, pp. 485-89; Burton, vi. 298-300; Stanley's *Church of Scotland*, p. 72. Burns quotes from Goldwin Smith (*Irish History and Irish Character*, p. 196) the remark that "nothing contributed more than the distinct national character and distinct religion of the Scotch, to save Britain from being entirely subjugated by the absolutism of Strafford and the Anglicanism of Laud. It was not in London, but in Edinburgh, that those conspirators first encountered serious resistance."

32. Cunningham's *Church of Scotland*, i. 526; ii. 40, 43, 45. On the eve of the outbreak of rebellion in England, the General Assembly sent a sympathetic communication to Parliament, and in 1643, after the outbreak, the Solemn League and Covenant was adopted which constituted the alliance between the Scottish Church and the English Parliament. Both in this Covenant and in the earlier National Covenant of 1638, distinct expressions of loyalty to the person and office of the King are united with a determination to resist royal oppression. One of the objects of the National Covenant is declared to be "maintaining the King's Majesty, his person and estate; and the signatories expressly repudiate "rebellion," and any attempt

at "diminution of the King's greatness and authority." The subscribers to the Solemn League and Covenant, while declaring their resolution to "preserve the rights and privileges of the Parliament, and the liberties of the kingdoms," and to accomplish the "preservation of the reformed religion in Scotland," as well as the "extirpation of prelacy," and the "reformation of religion in England and Ireland," are careful also to state their purpose to "preserve and defend the King's Majesty and authority." Regarding the attitude of the Church of England and her clergy (prior to the accession of James II.), see Lecky's *England in the Eighteenth Century*, i. pp. 8, 9; and Macaulay's *Hist. of Eng.* i. 60, 185; ii. 296; iii. 40, 41 (cab. ed.) "Her (the Church's) favourite theme was the doctrine of non-resistance. That doctrine she taught without any qualification, and followed out to all its extreme consequences."

33. Reid's *Presbyterian Church in Ireland*, ii. 409, 438-41, 449, 458; Hamilton's *Irish Presbyterian Church*, pp. 86, 103, 104; Macaulay, iv. 150, 159, 210, 229.

34. Hodge's *Presbyterian Church*, ii. 398, 399; Briggs's *American Presbyterianism*, pp. 347-51; Ellis Thompson's *Presbyterian Churches* in the United States, pp. 56, 57. In 1774, "a prominent advocate of the British Government" in America, "ascribed the revolt and revolution mainly to the action of the Presbyterian clergy and laity as early as 1764" (Hodge). Another contemporary on the same side writes, "I fix all the blame of these extraordinary American proceedings upon them" (the Presbyterians). "The Scoto-Irish on the frontiers of Virginia and North Carolina were the first to advance to a declaration of independence" (Briggs). The Rector of Trinity Church, New York, wrote in 1776, "I do not

know one of them (the Presbyterian ministers), nor have I been able, after strict inquiry, to hear of any, who did not, by preaching and every effort in their power, promote all the measures of Congress, however extravagant" (Briggs).

35. Buckle's *Civilisation in England*, i. 664-70, 847-50; Lecky's *England in the Eighteenth Century*, v. 301. Buckle gives ample evidence for his assertion that the great Frenchmen of the eighteenth century were stimulated by the example of England into a love of progress, and that it was English literature which taught the lessons of political liberty first to France, and through France to the rest of Europe. Lecky (as well as Buckle) shows how "English notions of liberty were made familiar to the French public" through the visits of eminent Frenchmen to Britain, and the translation of English works into French. Among French Revolutionists who travelled in Scotland was Marat, who received the degree of M.D. from St. Andrews University.

36. Bede's *Eccles. Hist.* iii. 25, 26.

37. Fordun's *Annals*, lix.; Cunningham's *Church of Scotland*, i. 114, 115; Stephen's *Scottish Church*, i. 353, 386.

38. Spoken in 1596, on the occasion of the royal proposal to recall the "popish lords" from exile (Cunningham, i. 432).

39. Cunningham, ii. 15, 187; Stephen, ii. 273, 434.

40. Cf. Lectures III. p. 81; V. p. 138.

41. See M'George in Story's *Church of Scotland*, iv. 124; cf. pp. 102, 103.

42. *Ibid.* pp. 104-107; and *Leading Ecclesiastical*

Cases decided in the Court of Session, 1849-74 (collected and edited by Mr. T. G. Murray), pp. 1-62.

44. See speech of Mr. Gladstone in the House of Commons on 6th July 1874, in the debate on the Patronage Bill of that year. "He protested against the power given to the Courts of the Church of Scotland, as a power not given to other Presbyterian bodies, and one that was entrusted to no other ecclesiastical tribunal in any other country." Cf. Dr. Arch. Scott, in *St. Giles's Lectures on the Scottish Church*, p. 340.

45. Ogilvie's *Presbyterian Churches*, pp. 61, 62, 63, 78, 91.

46. See Prof. Lechler's article on the "German Movement towards Presbytery" in the *Catholic Presbyterian* for February 1879. "Those evangelical churches of Germany in which elders are elected, church-sessions held, and synods of ministers and elders periodically assembled, count a population of about twenty millions of souls."

Addition to Note 35 on Lecture III.

As regards John Macleod Campbell, see *Memoir* by his son, Rev. Donald Campbell, M.A., vol. i. 212, 338; ii. 339; and *Life of F. D. Maurice* by his son, i. 183; ii. 537.

INDEX

ABOLITIONISTS, American, 272
Absolutism in Britain, 188, 281
Adair, Patrick, 96
Adolphus, Gustavus, 125, 153
Adopting Act, 153
Aidan, St., 10, 12, 18-21, 23, 27
Airth, William, 247
Aitchison, Sir Charles, 218
Alane, Alexander (Alesius), 112-115, 249, 250
Alison, Francis, 152, 268
America, Episcopal Church of, 137, 260
   Presbyterian Church of, 145-47, 151, 153, 154, 157
American Independence, 151, 162, 189, 190, 282
Amyraut, Amyraldists, 121
Anglicanism, 68, 164, 193, 282
Anglicans in North America, 161
Anglo-Catholic revival, 80, 198
Annesley, Samuel, 232
Anselm, 106
Anti-burgher Synod, 266
Aquinas, Thomas, 107, 108, 243
Arianism, 77, 78, 99, 155, 228, 229, 269
Armada, Spanish, 63, 128
Arminianism, 120, 121, 155

Arnold, Dr., quoted, 180
Articles, the Forty-two, 68
Arya Somaj, quoted, 54
Augustine, St., of Canterbury, 9, 12, 19-21, 23
Augustus (of Brunswick), 125
Australia, Presbyterian Church of, 133, 134
Awakening, the Great, 152, 154

BAILLIE, R., 227
Baliols, the, 172, 275, 278
Bancroft, American historian, quoted, 143, 263
Bancroft, Archbishop, 72
Bangor, monastery of, 14, 15, 207
Bannockburn, battle of, 173, 175, 180, 184
Baptists in America, 136, 161-63, 260
   Missionary Society of, 212
Barbour, John, 175
Basel, Council of, 244
Baxter, Richard, 125
Beale, Ninian, 141
Bean, St., 25
Beaton, David, 221, 245, 249
   James, 247
Beattie, Dr., 79, 230

286 SCOTTISH CHURCH IN CHRISTENDOM

Becon, quoted, 223
Bede's opinion of St. Aidan, 21
   of St. Columba, 208
Bernard, St., 106, 108, 243
Berno, 23
Beza, on Andrew Melville, 119
"Black Rubric," 68, 223
Blair, Hugh, 91
   Robert, 91, 236-38
Blane, St., 206
Boniface VIII., Pope, 173
   St., 17-19, 22, 23
Borland, Francis, 210
Bosa, Bishop, 205
Bothwell Bridge, battle of, 141, 261
Bower, quoted, 172
Bradburn, Samuel, 83
Brahmanism, 44, 47, 50
Brahmo Somaj, 54
Brainerd, David, 32-36, 211
Brendan, 14
Brice, Edward, 90, 91, 235, 237
Brisbane, Sir Thomas, 134
Brown, John, of Haddington, 229
   Samuel, of Birmingham, 228
Bruce, Robert, 1, 105, 170. 173, 175, 176, 275, 277, 278
Brude, King, 8
Bryce, Dr., of Calcutta, 214
Buchanan, George, 111, 112, 116, 182, 189, 248-49, 279
   Patrick, 249
Buddhism, 50
Buitt, St., 204
Buonaventura, 243
Burgher Synod, 266
Burnet, Bishop, on John Forbes of Corse, 255
Burns, Robert, 3
Burton on Duns Scotus, 243

CADROE, ST., 24-26, 110, 208
Caird, Principal, 230
Calderwood, David, 184
Calixtus, 125
Calvin, 129, 187
Calvinism—
   in France, 121, 253
   in Germany, 114, 124
   in United States, 162
Cameron, John, 120, 236, 253, 254
Cameronites, 121, 122
Campbell, Principal, of Aberdeen, 79
   Professor, of Glasgow, 155, 270
Canada, Presbyterian Church of, 158-60
Candida Casa (Whithorn), 5, 86
Canons, Scottish Book of, 280
Cappel, quoted, 121
Cardross, Lord, 142, 262
Carey, William, 38, 39, 44, 46, 47, 213, 215
Carlyle, Thomas, 3, 70, 186
Carmichael, Alexander, 76
   John, 245
Carstares, 187
Cartwright, Thomas, 226
Cathaldus, St., 207
Catholic League, 63, 127, 128, 220
Catholics, Roman, in England, 62
   in Ireland, 89
   in Scotland, 64
   in United States, 162
Cedda, St., 10
Chad, St., 10
Chalmers, Thomas, 78, 80
Charles I., 73, 93, 140, 185
Christmas, observance of, 183

INDEX

Church Missionary Society, 39
  State support of, 197
  See America, Australia, etc.
Civil War in Britain, 186, 280
Clarendon, Earl of, 260
Clonard, monastery of, 207
Cochlaeus, 250
Cole, John, 70, 225
College, Bishop's, 46, 215
  Carey's, 46
  Hindoo, 44
  Huguenot, 118, 121
  "Log," 152
  Presbyterian, in America, 152, 156
  Presbyterian, in Canada, 160
  Scots, 105, 174, 241, 248, 251
  Scottish Catholic, 251
Colmoc, St., 204
Colonial Scheme, 159
Colonisation, Scottish, 2, 88, 94, 103, 132, 145, 233
Columba, St., 7-9, 12-14, 16, 23, 27, 167, 204, 205
Columban Church, 16
Columbanus, St., 15
Colville, John, 253
Conall, King, 167
Commissioners, Scottish, to Ireland, 96
Communion, posture at, 67, 68, 124, 183, 223
Comyn, 175, 176, 275, 278
Confessions of Faith, 29, 157, 271
Comgall, 14
Congregationalists, 55, 219, 260, 261
Congress, American, 151, 166
Consensus, Swiss, 124
Consistories, 198
Constantine, King of Scotland, 25, 26, 208

Constitutional government of England, 177
Continental Aid Society, 129, 257
Conventicle Act, 76
Convocation, 82, 232
Cooke, Henry, 99
Copland, Patrick, 139
Cormach, 14
Coronel of Segovia, 248
Cotton, Bishop, quoted, 50
Covenanters, 32, 73, 75, 76, 93, 141, 186, 187, 261
Covenant, National, 122, 185, 188
Coverdale, 70, 225
Cranmer, 68, 69
Cromwell, Oliver, 31, 96, 140, 239
Crusade, tithe for, 193
Culdees, 86
Culdreivny, battle of, 204
Cumberland Presbyterian Church, 271
Cunningham, Robert, 90, 235, 237
Cuthbert, St., 10

DALRIADA, 167, 205, 206
Danish Bible, 115
  Church, 115
Darien Expedition, 32, 143, 210
D'Aubigné, Merle, 129, 257
Davenant, Bishop, 255
David, Bishop of Moray, 105, 174
Dickson of Edinburgh, 184
Discipline, English Book of, 72
  Scottish Book of, 72
Disruption in Scottish Church, 195
Divine right of kings, 188

Dominican friars, 66, 108
Donaldson, Walter, 120, 253
Duff, Alexander, 40, 42-54, 214, 215, 217, 218
Dunbar, battle of, 140
George, 91, 236
Duncan, Andrew, 118, 251
Dundee, Council of, 173, 277
Durie, John, 122-26, 255
Robert, 118, 251
Dutch Church, 118, 133
Independence, 209

EAST India Company, 38, 39
Education Acts, 200
Christian, in India, 46, 47, 52
Edward I., 169, 171-73, 178, 279
III., 170, 178
VI., 66
Edwards, Jonathan, 36
Eliot, John, 33
Elizabeth, Queen, 64, 68, 70, 127, 225
Ellis, Robert, 245
Emigration, English, to North America, 140
Irish, to North America, 144, 145, 158, 264
Scottish, to France, 104
Scottish, to Ireland, 90, 99, 150, 235, 239
Scottish, to North America, 141, 142, 158
England, Church of, 61, 63-65, 79, 81, 169, 187, 230, 238, 273, 286
English Presbyterianism, 76-79, 85, 230
Episcopate, Scottish, 81, 138, 171, 172
Erastianism, 81, 195, 198, 199

Erskine, John, 36
Establishment, Church, 192, 199
Ethelbert, King, 20
Evangelical Alliance, 126, 256
Evangelicals, English, 39, 229
Evangelisation of Africa, 55-60
of England, 9
of India, 45-54
of Scotland, 12, 129, 256
of Switzerland, 15

FAELAN, St., 204
Falconer, Bishop, 231
Finian, St., 86
Five Mile Act, 76
Forbes, John, of Alford, 118, 251
of Corse, 122, 123, 254, 255
Patrick, 118
Foreman, Andrew, 245
Foxe, 70, 225
France, Scots in, 104-108
Scottish alliance with, 104, 178
Franciscans, 244, 249
Frazer, John, 142, 263
Free Church of Scotland, 38, 195, 230
French Protestant Church, 118, 120, 198, 253
Protestant theology, 122
Fridoline, 15
Froude, quoted, 1

GADDERAR, Bishop, 231
Gallus, St., 15
General Assembly of Scottish Church, 32, 36, 43, 74, 83, 148, 155, 184, 193, 194, 196, 210, 211, 214, 265, 269, 270, 281

INDEX

General Assembly of American Church, 267
of Victorian Church, 259
General Presbyterian Council, 130, 257, 259
Geneva, Book of, 71
translation of the Bible, 225
German Church, 126, 198, 258
Gerson, 111
Gilby, 70, 225
Gillespie, George, 151, 227, 267
Glasgow Assembly of 1638, 186
Missionary Society, 37, 212
Synod of, 148
Goodman, Christopher, 225
Gregory the Great, 9, 273
Grotius, 125

HALDANE, Robert, 129, 256, 257
Hall, Bishop, 120, 255
Hamilton, James, 91, 236, 238
Patrick, 113, 237, 247
Hampton Court Conference, 227
"Harry Blind," quoted, 170, 275
Henderson, Alexander, 73, 74, 185, 227
Henry II. of England, 273
V., 178
VIII., 65, 220
Abbot of Arbroath, 172
Hermann von Wied, 113
High Commission, Court of, 185
Hilda, St., 10
Home Rule, 101
Hooper, Bishop, 223
Hugo of St. Victor, 106
Huguenots, 120, 252, 254, 270
Hume, David, 2, 45
Hundred Canons, Irish, 237
Hunter, Dr. Henry, 229

IMMACULATE conception, doctrine of, 107, 108, 243
Independence, American, 151, 158, 162, 189, 221
English, 179
Scottish, 1, 168-170
Scottish ecclesiastical, 169
spiritual, 199
Independents, English, 74
India, religion in, 44
missions in, 38-40, 45-54
Infallibility, Papal, 108
Inglis, Dr. John, 42, 45, 51, 100, 214
Iona, 7, 8, 9, 12-14, 16
Ireland, early Church of, 12, 16
Episcopal Church of, 91, 92
Presbyterian Church of, 89, 94, 95, 99, 100, 101
rebellion in, 94
saints of, on the Continent, 16

JACOBITES, 2, 195
James VI.'s ecclesiastical policy in Scotland, 30, 89, 90, 118, 119, 128, 184
Jesuits, 62, 63, 127
John of Beverley, 206
Jolly, Bishop, 80, 231
Jonston, John, quoted, 250

KENNETH, 14
Kilgour, Bishop, 138
Kilham, Alexander, 83, 232
Kilian, 15, 246
Kingdoms, union of, 77
Kirk-session in England, 72
Knox, John, 64, 66-69, 91, 116, 151, 181, 221, 223, 224 246, 247, 258

LAMBERTON, Bishop, 172-74
Lang, John Dunmore, 134, 258

Latimer, 224
Laud, Archbishop, 73, 92, 96, 140, 255, 260, 281
Leechman, 155, 270
Leighton, Dr. Alexander, 73, 140, 227
Leslie, Bishop, 117
Lever, Thomas, 224
Lightfoot, Bishop, quoted, 12
Lindisfarne, 10, 12, 20, 21, 23
Liturgy, English, 226
Laud's, 183, 185
Livingstone, David, 40, 54-60
John, 91, 237, 238
London Missionary Society, 38
Long Parliament, 74, 227
"Lord of the Isles," quoted, 176
Love, Dr. John, 38, 212
Luther, 113, 115,
Lutheranism, 114, 124, 247, 250

M'Alpine, John (Machabaeus), 66, 114, 221, 250
M'Brair, John, 66, 222
M'Dowel, John, 66, 221
Macfarlane, William, 41, 214
Mackay, Alexander, 41, 214
Macleod, Norman, 80, 230
M'Nish, George, 150, 266, 268
Major, John, 107, 110, 111, 113, 181, 241, 246-48
Makemie, Francis, 151, 266-68
Malan, Cesar, 129
Margaret, Queen, 87, 193
Marian persecution, 69
Mariolatry, 107
Mary Stewart, 61, 64, 91, 128
Tudor, 69
Massacre of St. Bartholomew, 128
Irish, 92, 238
Mayflower, The, 139

Mayhew, Thomas, 33
Medical missions, 52, 217
Melanchthon, 110, 113, 115, 248, 250
Melville, Andrew, 119, 120, 184, 193, 194, 252, 253, 255, 281
Mendicant friars, 110
Methodists, Methodism, 82-85, 136, 156, 161-63, 232, 260
Middleton, Bishop, 46
Millenary Petition, 72, 226
Miller, Principal, quoted, 254
Milligan, Dr. W., 80
Milton, John, 182, 254
Ministry, native Indian, 40, 53
Missions, American Presbyterian, 149, 160, 164, 209
Anglo-Saxon, 18
Colonial, 148
Danish, 212
Dutch, 209
Irish, 14, 16-18, 204, 206, 207
Moravian, 37, 211
Medical, 52, 217
Roman Catholic, 28, 29
Scottish, in America, 32, 148, 149, 211, 266
Scottish, in Africa, 38, 40, 41, 59, 212
"Scottish," on the Continent, 109, 110
Scottish, in England, 9-12
Scottish, in India, 38, 39, 41, 46, 216, 218
Swedish, 209
Swiss, 208
Missionary revival, 38-40
shortcomings, 28
societies in Scotland, 32, 37
Mochta, St., 204
Moderates, Moderatism, 151, 155, 214, 267

INDEX

Moffat, Robert, 40, 213
Monasteries and monks, Benedictine, 109, 116, 245
  Irish, 13-16, 86, 245
  Scottish, 10, 109, 116, 246
Monastic reform, 247
Monday, Thanksgiving, 229, 237
Monod Frederick, 129
Montalembert on Scottish monks, 11
Morrison, Robert, 40, 213
Morton, Regent, 193
Munro, General, 94

NANTES, Edict of, 270
National Churches, 198, 199
  Covenant, 73, 281
  movement under Wallace and Bruce, 173
New Connexion, Methodist, 84, 233
"New Side" in American Presbyterian Church, 154, 156
New York, Synod of, 145-47
Ninian, St., 5, 86
Norham Convention, 171
Norman Conquest, 245
Northampton, Council of, 169
  Treaty of, 170
Nye, Philip, 74

OATH of Allegiance to Edward I., 171, 275, 276
Occom, Samson, 149
Odo, of Clugny, 24
"Old Side" in American Presbyterian Church, 154, 269
Ordination formula in American Presbyterian Church, 153, 157
Orientalists in India, 49, 216
Oswald, King, 9

Oxford Movement, 231

PACIFIC Act, Irish, 269
Papal Bull recognising independence of Scottish Church, 170
  excommunication of Bruce, 175
  legates excluded from Scotland, 193
Paris, University of, 105
Pastoral Letter on missions, 43
Paton, John Gibson, 41, 135, 213
Patrick, St., 5, 6, 85, 204
Patriotism, Scottish, 2, 103, 169, 171, 173, 175, 184
Patronage, abolition of, 196
Peden, Alexander, 76
Pelagianism in English Presbyterian Church, 228
Pentland Rising, 261
Perth Articles, 185
Petrie, Bishop, 138
Philadelphia, Synod of, 146, 148
"Pilgrim Fathers," 139
Pius V., Pope, 220
  IX., Pope, 108, 224
"Plea against Prelacy," Leighton's, 73
Poor Laws, 200
Potitus, of Strathclyde, 5
Prelacy, opposition to, 73, 227
Presbyterianism, African, 133
  American, 137-57, 161-66, 259, 270
  Australian, 134, 258, 259
  Canadian, 158-61, 271
  English, 73-79
  Irish, 87-101, 233-39
  New Zealand, 135
  Scottish, 71, 75, 79, 82, 85, 118, 119, 147, 149, 187

Presbyterians, Scottish, in France, 118
in Holland, 118
influence in America, 139, 140, 147, 157, 163
influence on English Presbyterians, 70, 78
Presbytery, earliest in America, 145
earliest in Australia, 134, 259
earliest in Ireland, 95
origin of Scottish, 71
"Presbytery" of Wandsworth, 72
Priestley, Joseph, 228, 229
Priests, Scottish, in exile, 116
Proctor, Henry, of Stafford, 229
Protestantism in Denmark, 115
in England, 62, 65, 127
in France, 120, 253
in Germany, 114
in Ireland, 87, 89
in Scotland, 62, 64, 66, 128
in United States, 161
Puritans, Puritanism in America, 139, 164
in England, 33, 65-73, 225, 226, 229
manifesto issued at Geneva by John Knox, 70
worship, 68

Ramsay, William, 249
Ratisbon, conference at, 114
Scottish monastery of, 109, 117
Rattray, Bishop, 231
Rebellion in Ireland, 92-94, 238
Rectors, Scottish, in Paris University, 109
Reformation, Danish, 115, 221

Reformation, English, 64, 127
German, 113, 114
Irish, 89
Scottish, 62, 65, 70, 113, 220, 225, 258
difference between English and Scottish, 64
influence of Scottish on England, 70, 71
Reformers, Scottish, in England, 66
on the Continent, 112-15
Refugees, English Protestant, on the Continent, 70
Reid, Thomas, 2, 79
Renwick, James, 32, 187
Restoration of 1660, a reaction, 75, 187
Reunion, ecclesiastical, in America, 152, 157, 160
in Australia, 134
in Germany, 124, 126
in Ireland, 239
Revolution, American, 138, 162, 190, 191
British, 76, 183, 188-90
French, 190, 191, 283
Revival, Evangelical, in America, 154
in England, 79
in Scotland, 78
missionary, 40
Riddell, Archibald, 142, 262
Riot in St. Giles's, 185
Robertson, Principal, 3, 156, 214
Romanism in North America, 260
conspiracy to restore, in Britain, 62, 127
Rothes, Lord, 185
Rough, John, 66, 221

INDEX

SAGE, Bishop, 231
St. Clair, Bishop, 174
St. Victor, Richard of, 106, 241
Sampson, 70, 225
San Romano, instructed by M'Alpine, 115
Sarum, use of, 171, 275
Schism, earliest in American Presbyterian Church, 152, 154-57
Scots College, 105, 174, 241, 248
  Guard, 104, 240
  Presbytery in London, 229
Scottish Church, see *Contents*
Scottish Missionary Society, 212
"Scottizing" in England, 72
Scotus, Duns, 106-108, 241-44
Seabury, Bishop, 81, 138, 260
Secession, American, 160
  English, 71
  Irish, 239
  Scottish, 99, 149, 158, 160, 195, 229, 230, 239
Senalis, 248
Seton, Alexander, 66, 221
Sharp, John, 118, 251
Shields, Alexander, 32, 210
Shotts Revival, 237
Simeon, Charles, of Cambridge, 39
Simson, Professor, of Glasgow, 155, 228, 270
Skinner, Bishop John, 80, 138
Slave traffic, African, 57
Smith, Adam, 2
  Robertson, 80
  Sydney, 39
Society for Propagation of Christian knowledge, 32, 42, 148, 149, 210, 266

Socinians, 77, 228, 229
Solemn League and Covenant, 74, 91, 95, 122, 281, 282
Spiritual independence, 119, 192
Stanley, Dean, on Scottish theologians, 230
Star Chamber, 140, 227
Stewart dynasty, despotism of, 1, 183-88
Stirke, George, 139, 260
Stirling, Principal, 149, 150
Strachan, Bishop, 271
Strafford, 92, 96, 186, 281

TAYLOR, Jeremy, 97
  John, 228
Tennent, William, 152, 154, 268
Ternan, 86
Test Act, Irish, 144
Thirty-nine Articles, 68
Thirty Years' War, 123, 128, 170
Thomas, missionary in India, 38, 213
Thomson, Dr. Andrew, 78
Toleration Act, 268
Transubstantiation, 247, 249
Trevelyan, Sir Charles, on Duff 51
Trudpert, 15
Tyrconnel, Earl of, 88
Tyrone, Earl of, 88
Tulloch, Principal, 80, 230

ULSTER, prosperity of, 87, 233
Uniformity, Act of, 75
United Presbyterian Church, 38, 230
University of Coimbra, 112
  Paris, 105, 108
  Scottish, 78, 145
Ussher, Archbishop, 92, 125, 234

Vasa, Gustavus, 209
Vatican Council, 108
Veitch, William, 76
Villegagnon, 208
Voluntaryism, 165, 195
Vossius, 125

Waldensian Church, 130
Walker, Bishop, of Edinburgh, 81
Wallace, Gabriel, 116
   William, 1, 172, 276, 278
Wars of Scottish Independence, 1, 168
Watt, James, 3
Waverley, 3
"Weekly Exercise," 71
Welsh, John, 91, 118, 236, 237, 251
   Josias, 91
Wentworth, *see* Strafford

Wesley, 82, 83
Westminster Assembly, 74
   Confession, 77, 124, 153, 269
White, John, 232, 255
Whitefield, George, 34, 152-56, 268
Whittingham, 70, 225
Wigbert, 18
Wilberforce, Bishop Samuel, 232
Wilfrid, 10, 11, 18, 206
Willebrord, 18
William of Orange, 188
   the Lion, 273
Willock, John, 66, 221
Wilson, John, 41, 213
Wishart, Bishop, 172, 174, 277
   Principal, 155, 229, 270
Witherspoon, Dr. John, 151, 190, 207
Wordsworth, Bishop, quoted, 231

THE END

Printed by R. & R. Clark, Limited, *Edinburgh*.

In Crown 8vo, Cloth. Price 7s. 6d. net.

STUDIES IN
HEBREW PROPER NAMES

BY

G. BUCHANAN GRAY, M.A.

LECTURER IN HEBREW AND OLD TESTAMENT THEOLOGY IN MANSFIELD COLLEGE;
LATE SENIOR KENNICOTT SCHOLAR IN THE UNIVERSITY OF OXFORD.

In Crown 8vo, Cloth. Price 7s. 6d. net.

THE
APOCALYPSE OF BARUCH

TRANSLATED FROM THE SYRIAC

BY

REV. R. H. CHARLES

AUTHOR OF 'THE BOOK OF ENOCH,' ETC.

A. & C. BLACK, SOHO SQUARE, LONDON.

In Demy 8vo, Cloth. Price 24s.

INTRODUCTION

TO THE

BOOK OF ISAIAH

WITH AN APPENDIX CONTAINING THE UNDOUBTED
PORTIONS OF THE TWO CHIEF PROPHETIC
WRITERS IN A TRANSLATION

BY

The REV. T. K. CHEYNE, M.A., D.D.

ORIEL PROFESSOR OF THE INTERPRETATION OF HOLY SCRIPTURE AT OXFORD,
AND FORMERLY FELLOW OF BALLIOL COLLEGE; CANON OF ROCHESTER.

"This elaborate and scholarly work. . . . We must leave to professed scholars the detailed appreciation of Professor Cheyne's work. His own learning and reputation suffice to attest its importance."—*The Times.*

"Full of learning, and forms a perfect mine of critical research."—*National Observer.*

"This truly great and monumental work."—*Critical Review.*

"We heartily congratulate the author on the completion of a long projected work, which will at once take its place among the most important on its subject."—*Primitive Methodist Quarterly Review.*

"A further and notable contribution to the study of the interesting and difficult problems presented by the Book of Isaiah."—*Baptist Magazine.*

"This monument of patient scholarship, wide reading, and indefatigable research."—*The Speaker.*

"Ein ausgezeichnetes Werk! Des Verfassers kritische Kraft, seine Umsicht in der Untersuchung und die besonnene Ruhe seines Urtheils, insbesondere aber auch die ungewöhnliche Klarheit seiner Darstellung, die auch die verwickeltsten Fragen in angenehmster Form darzubieten vermag, haben längst schon seinen Namen bei den Fachgenossen hochangesehen gemacht."—*Deutsche Litteratur Zeitung.*

A. & C. BLACK, SOHO SQUARE, LONDON.

WORKS BY THE LATE W. ROBERTSON SMITH, M.A., LL.D.
Professor of Arabic in the University of Cambridge

Demy 8vo. Price 15s. net.

LECTURES ON THE RELIGION OF THE SEMITES

THE FUNDAMENTAL INSTITUTIONS

New Edition. Revised throughout by the Author

Demy 8vo. Price 10s. 6d.

THE OLD TESTAMENT IN THE JEWISH CHURCH

A COURSE OF LECTURES ON BIBLICAL CRITICISM

Second Edition. Revised and much Enlarged

Post 8vo. Price 10s. 6d.

THE PROPHETS OF ISRAEL

AND THEIR PLACE IN HISTORY

To the Close of the Eighth Century B.C.

Second Edition

WITH INTRODUCTION AND ADDITIONAL NOTES

BY

The REV. T. K. CHEYNE, M.A., D.D.

ORIEL PROFESSOR OF THE INTERPRETATION OF HOLY SCRIPTURE AT OXFORD
CANON OF ROCHESTER

A. & C. BLACK, SOHO SQUARE, LONDON

A SHORT HISTORY OF SYRIAC LITERATURE

By The Late WILLIAM WRIGHT, LL.D., Professor of Arabic in the University of Cambridge.

Crown 8vo. Price 6s. net.

SKETCH OF THE HISTORY OF ISRAEL AND JUDAH

By J. WELLHAUSEN, Professor at Marburg.

Third Edition. Crown 8vo. Price 5s.

SKETCHES FROM EASTERN HISTORY

By THEODOR NÖLDEKE, Professor of Oriental Languages in the University of Strassburg. Translated by JOHN SUTHERLAND BLACK, M.A., LL.D., and revised by the Author.

Demy 8vo. Price 10s. 6d.

NATURAL THEOLOGY

THE GIFFORD LECTURES

DELIVERED BEFORE THE UNIVERSITY OF EDINBURGH

FIRST COURSE 1891 ; SECOND COURSE 1893

By Professor Sir G. G. STOKES, Bart., M.P.

Crown 8vo. Price 3s. 6d. each.

OLD TESTAMENT THEOLOGY

OR

THE HISTORY OF HEBREW RELIGION

FROM THE YEAR 800 B.C.

By ARCHIBALD DUFF, M.A., LL.D., Professor of Old Testament Theology in the Yorkshire United Independent College, Bradford.

Demy 8vo. Price 10s. 6d.

THE MEMORABILIA OF JESUS

COMMONLY CALLED THE GOSPEL OF ST. JOHN

By Rev. W. W. PEYTON

Post 8vo. Price 10s. 6d.

A. & C. BLACK, SOHO SQUARE, LONDON.

THE
LIVES OF THE FATHERS
SKETCHES OF CHURCH HISTORY IN BIOGRAPHY

BY

FREDERIC W. FARRAR, D.D., F.R.S.
DEAN OF CANTERBURY

2 Vols. Demy 8vo. Price 24s.

THE LIFE OF CHRIST
AS REPRESENTED IN ART.

BY

FREDERIC W. FARRAR, D.D., F.R.S.
DEAN OF CANTERBURY

New Edition, containing all the Illustrations which appeared in the large Edition.

Post 8vo. Price 10s. 6d.

A. & C. BLACK, SOHO SQUARE, LONDON.

GUILD TEXT-BOOKS.

Price 6d. each net.

LANDMARKS OF CHURCH HISTORY.
By Prof. COWAN, D.D., University of Aberdeen. Seventeenth Thousand.

RELIGIONS OF THE WORLD.
By Principal GRANT, D.D., Queen's University, Canada. Eighteenth Thousand.

OUR LORD'S TEACHING.
By Rev. J. ROBERTSON, D.D., Whittinghame. Tenth Thousand.

HISTORY OF THE ENGLISH BIBLE.
By Rev. GEORGE MILLIGAN, B.D., Caputh. Tenth Thousand.

THE CHURCH OF SCOTLAND. A Sketch of its History.
By Rev. P. M'ADAM MUIR, D.D., Edinburgh. Nineteenth Thousand.

LIFE AND CONDUCT.
By Very Rev. J. CAMERON LEES, D.D., LL.D., Dean of the Chapel Royal of Scotland. Twentieth Thousand.

CHRISTIAN EVIDENCES.
By Very Rev. ALEXANDER STEWART, D.D., Principal of St. Mary's College, St. Andrews. Seventeenth Thousand.

THE NEW TESTAMENT AND ITS WRITERS.
By Rev. J. A. M'CLYMONT, D.D., Aberdeen. Twenty-ninth Thousand.

THE OLD TESTAMENT AND ITS CONTENTS.
By Prof. ROBERTSON, D.D., University of Glasgow. Seventeenth Thousand.

EXPOSITION OF THE APOSTLES' CREED.
By Rev. J. DODDS, D.D., Corstorphine.

THE PRESBYTERIAN CHURCHES. Their Place and Power in Modern Christendom.
By Rev. J. N. OGILVIE, M.A., Bangalore.

A. & C. BLACK, SOHO SQUARE, LONDON.

www.ingramcontent.com/pod-product-compliance
Lightning Source LLC
Chambersburg PA
CBHW030016240426
43672CB00007B/969